COLLINS STUDY SKILLS IN ENGLISH

Listening Comprehension & Note-taking Course

K James
R R Jordan
A J Matthews

with *Alternative Guided Note-taking*
and *Follow-up activities* by
J P O'Brien

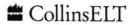 CollinsELT

A Division of HarperCollins*Publishers*

Collins ELT
HarperCollins Publishers
77–85 Fulham Palace Rd
Hammersmith, London W6 8JB

© K. James, R. R. Jordan and A. J. Matthews, 1979
© K. James, R. R. Jordan, A. J. Matthews and J. P. O'Brien, 1991

First published 1979
This revised and enlarged edition first published 1991

Printed in Great Britain by
Scotprint Ltd., Musselburgh

ISBN 0 00 370781 4

This book is accompanied by a set of 2 cassettes.

Authors' acknowledgements
We are grateful to the following for their assistance with the production of this course:
Jane Jordan and Gerry Abbott for their help with recording; Terry McMylor for recording
and editing the tapes; Barbara Wilkinson for typing the manuscript. We should also like
to express our gratitude to the following for assistance with pilot versions of the texts and
exercises and for feedback on using the Units: Ian Anderson, Ann Brown, Molly Winder,
Andrew Thomas, Graham Cawood, Ruth Nixon and Donald Sim. We are indebted to
numerous overseas students at the University of Manchester for whom most of the material
in this course was originally composed. We wish to express our sincere thanks to Gordon
Jarvie for his sympathetic encouragement and help with the editing of the course.
    We are grateful to the following for permission to reproduce the photographs as listed:
E. Barber, "Teaching English to Speakers of Other Languages" © The British Council 1989
(page 31); Sally & Richard Greenhill Photo-Library (pages 15, 47, 55, 63, 71, 79); Nigel
Luckhurst (page 39); Janine Wiedel Photo-Library (pages 23, 87).

List of Contents

* against some exercises above indicates an 'open-ended' exercise

INTRODUCTION

The Aims of the Course

1 To enable the non-native speaker of English who wishes to follow a course in the medium of English at tertiary level to:
   (a) follow a lecture on a non-specialized topic delivered in a neutral style by speakers from different backgrounds;
   (b) write adequate notes on such a lecture.
2 To provide useful information and to stimulate interest in the language learning and the study skills appropriate for such a student.

Methods

The methods for this course, which consists of this workbook together with an integral set of two cassettes, have resulted from various theoretical insights and from an extended period of testing of an experimental course design.

Note-taking is a highly complex skill consisting of three major components:
   (i) decoding
   (ii) comprehending
   (iii) writing what is important.
Each of these components needs to be developed if progress is to be made.

Accurate and comprehensive decoding is particularly crucial at the beginning of a lecture when the context is weak and when the student is 'tuning in' to the lecturer's voice. This is also the part of the talk where the lecturer normally states his/her intentions as to what will be covered and how it will be treated. It may often be vital for the student to make detailed notes here.

Stage 1 of each Unit of work, therefore, provides a simulated overview of a lecture ($\frac{1}{2}-\frac{3}{4}$ minute in length) on which work is done to develop accurate decoding. This is treated mainly as a dictation exercise in which the accurate recognition of such features as weak forms, contractions, vowel reduction, 'difficult' phonemes etc. may be dealt with in a meaningful context. (Further work is done on this at Stage 2 with Exercise 2: Blank-filling.)

Stage 2 of each Unit, an intermediary text (between the Stage 1 overview and the Stage 3 lecturette), is exploited in order to develop the global and the detailed comprehension necessary for effective note-taking. A *native-speaker* in a lecture situation is able to understand and process information at the required speed and density for many reasons. The most important is, perhaps, the extent of his/her ability to predict both grammatically and semantically.

The exercises at Stage 2 level, therefore, try to strengthen the student's fluency and accuracy in key grammatical structures, make him/her aware when and how they are used and inculcate the habit of searching for global and specific meaning.

Stage 3 of each Unit gives the necessary practice in taking notes. The *Guided Note-taking* exercise will, it is hoped, encourage the student to develop an ability to:
   (1) select the important points
   (2) choose an appropriate time to write them
   (3) write them succinctly and quickly
   (4) lay them out clearly.
This is done through providing some, but by no means all, of the main points and requiring the student to complete the remainder. Initial practice in these operations is provided in the section on *How to Take Notes*. The *Suggested Notes* (in the Key) will give an opportunity for the student to compare his/her notes and to discuss alternative answers with the teacher.

In this New Edition, an additional or alternative approach to taking notes is presented (*Alternative Guided Note-taking*): this requires the student to recognize the typical oral signals that precede the lecturer's key points. A list of *Follow-up Activities* is also suggested: including requesting clarification, rectifying omissions, oral reconstruction, written summary and discussion of content.

The authors have found that these materials have been consistently evaluated in formal feedback sessions by 85–90% of their students as being 'very valuable' or 'valuable' in helping them to develop their note-taking skills in lectures. They seem to value particularly the systematic and balanced way in which *decoding*, *comprehending* and *writing what is important* are dealt with.

HOW TO USE THE BOOK

To the Teacher and Student

Firstly, the *content* and sequence of the various exercises in the Units of the Course are described. This is followed by a brief description of the *Key to the Exercises*. Finally, there are detailed instructions and suggestions for *using the Units*. In general, we recommend that the procedures are followed, but a virtue of the course is that it is *flexible*. Thus, after completing perhaps Units 1 and 2 in full, more advanced students may consider omitting Stage 1. Alternatively, after Units 1 and 2, the teacher may experiment by starting at Stage 3 and finishing with the Stage 2 exercises. All students should read the section *How to Take Notes* before commencing the *Guided Note-taking/Alternative Guided Note-taking* exercises at Stage 3 level.

Content of Units

> ### STAGE 1

> | | |
> |---|---|
> | *Dictation* | This intensive listening exercise provides a summary of <u>Stage 2</u> and simulates an 'overview' of a lecture. |

> ### STAGE 2

> | | |
> |---|---|
> | *Exercise 1* | *Listening Comprehension*
Five true/false questions provide a check on overall listening comprehension and summarize the important points. |
> | *Exercise 2* | *Listening and Blank-filling*
Text of the talk with spaces to be filled. An intensive listening exercise which provides a summary of <u>Stage 3</u> when completed. It focuses attention on weak forms of verbs, prepositions etc., contractions and other features of the spoken language. It also provides a check on sound/spelling relationships. |
> | *Exercise 3* | *Reading Comprehension*
Five true/false questions based on the Text (in Exercise 2) deal with detailed points. Written evidence (quotations from the Text) is required for the answers. |
> | *Exercise 4*
Exercise 5 | *Grammatical Exercises*
On a functional/structural basis key grammatical items employed in the talks are selected for recognition and written practice. |

> ### STAGE 3

> | | |
> |---|---|
> | *Guided Note-taking* | Guidance is given in the form of headings, cues and layout. This is completed as the 'full length' talk is listened to.
Initial guidance is given in the section *How To Take Notes*. |
> | *Alternative Guided Note-taking* | Alternative guidance is given in the form of a list of the 'signals' used by the lecturer together with the corresponding framework. |
> | *Follow-up Activities* | These provide for the checking of the students' notes through exercises in clarification, comprehension and oral reconstruction. They also include discussion and writing tasks and, where appropriate, study skills exercises based on the content of the talk. |

Key to the Exercises

STAGE 1	*Text* The complete text for dictation/checking.
	Notes These cover the important features of pronunciation, structure and vocabulary within the talk/text.
STAGE 2	*Key to the Exercises*
	Detailed answers to Exercises 1–5, together with some additional notes.
STAGE 3	*Suggested Notes*
	Completed notes for the talk are provided.
	Text The complete text for comparison with the talk/notes.
	The signals listed in the *Alternative Guided Note-taking* exercise are underlined to facilitate checking the notes.
	Follow-up Activities
	Detailed answers are provided where possible.

Using the Units

STAGE 1

Dictation
1 The students should *listen* to the tape (Stage 1 Text is in the *Key to the Exercises*) while it is played the first time.
2 The second time it is played they should write it as a *dictation*: the aim here is accuracy. If necessary the tape can be played a third time for checking.
3 The students should then compare their dictation with the Text (in the *Key to the Exercises*), correcting any mistakes themselves. As a final check the teacher should see the dictations.
4 Speech practice can be given by the students repeating after the voice on tape or reading the Text aloud (paying attention to stress, intonation and pronunciation).
5 The *Notes* (in the *Key to the Exercises*) can be used to help explain or understand difficulties or features of pronunciation, structure and vocabulary used in the talk.

STAGE 2

Exercise 1: Listening Comprehension
1 The students should turn to this exercise in the workbook, look at the questions and then try to answer them (True or False) while listening to the taped talk. (They should *not* yet look at Exercise 2 as it contains most of the text of the talk.) It may sometimes be necessary to play the tape twice to ensure general understanding.
2 Correct Exercise 1 *orally*. Replay the tape if necessary and the students can check their answers. The Text should *not* be looked at yet.

Exercise 2: Listening and Blank-filling
1 Play the taped talk again. The students should write in the missing words (many of them are 'weak forms' and 'contractions') as they listen to the tape. It may occasionally be necessary to stop the tape at the end of a sentence or paragraph to give the students time to write, or to play the tape (or parts of it) again.
2 The teacher should go through the answers with the students. The students should check their answers carefully (by looking in the *Key to the Exercises*): they should pay particular attention to the spelling, and correct their mistakes.
3 Items causing difficulty should be given oral–aural practice.

Exercise 3: Reading Comprehension
1 The questions should be read and then answered (True/False; with evidence from the Text) after carefully reading the completed Exercise 2 (which then provides the Text for this Stage).
2 The answers can be checked by looking in the *Key to the Exercises*. Some discussion may be necessary.

Exercise 4 and Exercise 5: Grammatical Exercises
1 Most of the exercises are carefully controlled and can, therefore, be written straightaway (though oral preparation may often be useful). Some of them may be given as homework.
2 A few, usually more open-ended, exercises would benefit from oral discussion, both before and after writing. (These are indicated in the Contents by *.)
3 Answers and suggestions are to be found in the *Key to the Exercises*.

STAGE 3

Guided Note-taking
1 The students should try to complete the spaces left for notes on the *Guided Note-taking* page as they listen carefully to the taped-talk. The use of abbreviations and symbols is explained in the section *How To Take Notes*.
2 It may be necessary to stop the tape at the end of some sentences or paragraphs in order to give the students time to write (though this should be done as infrequently as possible). It is important that the students do not attempt to write too much: they should write the minimum to give sufficient meaning. It may be necessary to play the tape (or parts of it) a second time for slower students.
3 The students should turn to the *Suggested Notes* in the *Key to the Exercises* and compare their own notes carefully with them, noting errors, omissions or differences, and checking with the teacher.
4 It may be profitable to re-play the talk and read the *Suggested Notes* at the same time, observing the structure of the notes.
5 The *Text* of the talk is contained in the *Key to the Exercises* and may be used for comparison with the notes or for clarifying any difficulties.
6 Extra writing practice may be provided by asking the students to write a summary of the talk based upon their notes (see *Follow-up Activities*).
7 Advanced students may try to write their own notes without the help of the *Guided Note-taking*. Note, however, that less guidance is given with the later Units. Also, see *Alternative Guided Note-taking*.
8 Teachers may care to explain or discuss some of the matters raised by the note-taking, e.g. why certain items are included and others excluded. They may also wish to demonstrate a 'live' note-taking session by writing notes on the board, or the O.H.P., while the lecture is being played. The class then discuss how effectively this has been done.
9 An advanced group will find it stimulating to listen to the *class teacher* produce the Stage 3 (full lecturette) talk *live* from the notes in the Key. This can be recorded while the lecture takes place.

Alternative Guided Note-taking
An alternative framework is provided for each Unit. The suggested procedures outlined below aim to achieve a gradual withdrawal of support.
Note:
   (i)   The students may find it helpful to do both note-taking exercises (i.e. the *Guided* and the *Alternative Guided Note-taking*) for the first two units, i.e. until they are more familiar with the mechanics of note-taking.
   (ii) The first part of Unit 1 has been done as an example.
   (iii) Generally, the two note-taking exercises are best treated as alternatives and the students should be discouraged from referring to the *Guided Note-taking* exercise whilst doing the *Alternative* exercise.

Procedure [A] (Units 1 and 3)
(1) Before playing the introductory section of the talk (i.e. the first paragraph of the *Text*), ask the students to listen for the topic and the outline.
(2) Discuss any suggestions.
(3) The students should now turn to the *Alternative Guided Note-taking* exercise and make a note of the topic in the appropriate place (this has already been done in Unit 1).
(4) Play the rest of the talk and ask the students to raise their hand or shout 'STOP' when they hear listed signals.

(5) At each instance, stop the cassette and ask the students to suggest what is likely to follow. The aim here is: (1) to assess the students' ability to recognize the signals, and (2) to check that they understand the function they serve.

(6) 'Recap' and ask the students to note down the point made.

(7) Play the talk a second time if necessary.

Procedure B (Units 2, 4 and 5)

(1) Write the title of the talk on the blackboard and ask the students to suggest what is likely to be included in the talk. Write up any suggestions.

(2) The students should turn to the *Alternative Guided Note-taking* page and note down the title as indicated.

(3) Play the talk and ask the students to listen and take notes using the list of signals to help them.

(4) The students should compare their notes with the content predicted before the talk (this should be done after *Follow-up Activity* (1)).

Procedure C (Units 6, 7 and 8)

Ask the students to cover the righthand side of the *Alternative Guided Note-taking* page and take notes using the signals only, i.e. devising their own framework.

Procedure D (Units 9 and 10)

The students should now try and take notes without using the *Alternative Guided Note-taking* page at all, listening very carefully for the signals.

Note: A very advanced class can reverse the order of the units: first producing their own notes from the Stage 3 talk without any help from the book; then going on to do the Stage 2 blank-filling and reading comprehension; and finally writing, unseen, an overview/introduction to the whole talk. This can be compared with other students' versions and with the overview printed in the Key.

Note: If two classes are following the course simultaneously ask each class to study a different Unit. Class A then presents it to Class B in a final lecture form, with each Class A member reconstructing a part of the talk, and each Class B member taking notes. Discussion and clarification sessions then take place. The process is then reversed.

Follow-up Activities

The main activity types described below are featured on a cyclical basis. Reference to each activity type is in fairly general terms since detailed procedural notes accompany the activities themselves.

1 Requesting Clarification (Units 1, 4, 9 and 10)
In Units 1 and 4, the student is required to request clarification from the class/teacher. In Units 9 and 10, a more informal strategy is introduced with the students working in pairs. This exercise lends itself to a focus on language.

2 Discussion (Units 1, 4, 7 and 9)
The main aim here is to encourage the student to interact with the content of the talks by drawing on his/her experiences.

3 Oral Reconstruction (Units 2, 5, 7, 9 and 10)
In Units 2, 5 and 7 the oral reconstruction of the talk from notes is used primarily as a checking device. The secondary aim of developing the student's ability to speak fluently and coherently from a set of notes is, however, given greater priority in Units 9 and 10. Here, oral reconstruction is preceded by a clarification exercise. Thus any omissions/ points of uncertainty should already have been resolved.

Note:
 (i) The teacher is advised to provide a model the first time this activity is used.
 (ii) As much feedback as possible should be provided on the student's performance.
 (iii) This type of exercise has been found to be particularly useful in preparing students for giving talks.

4 Comprehension Check (Units 3, 6 and 8)
In Units 3 and 6 the student is required to answer a number of questions from his/her notes. In Unit 8 it is the student who constructs questions around any omissions/points of uncertainty in his/her notes.

5 Writing (Units 2, 5, 6 and 10)
This activity consists of a progressively longer summary of the talk based on the student's notes.
   Unit 7 also incorporates the results of the discussion exercise.

6 Study Skills Tasks (Units 4, 6 and 8)
Unit 4: Dictionary Task. This seeks to introduce the student to the respective uses of the bilingual and monolingual dictionary. The starting point for the exercise is the problematic nature of translation as described in the talk.
Unit 6: Library Task. This focuses on the library catalogue card and, in a very limited way, introduces the student to his/her English language school or university library if he/she has access to one.
Unit 8: Asking Questions about a Text. This is rather more language-oriented and follows up a very valid point made in the talk, namely, the need to provide precise information about the location of any word, etc. requiring explanation.

7 Review of the Lecturer's Signals (Unit 3)
Here the student is encouraged to view the signals listed in each of the *Alternative Guided Note-taking* exercises as both a listening and a speaking aid. It is hoped through the exercise initiated in Unit 3 to provide the student with a 'bank' of useful language items for academic speaking.
   Note: The teacher will, of course, need to monitor the exercise periodically.

THE CASSETTES

There are 2 cassettes that accompany this workbook and they are an integral part of the course. They consist of 3 talks (Stages 1, 2, 3) for each of the 10 Units: they are simulated academic-type lectures, fairly formally delivered, having been very carefully prepared. The talks vary in length but on average Stage 1 is $\frac{1}{2}-\frac{3}{4}$ minute, Stage 2 is about 3 minutes and Stage 3 is about 8 minutes. Both male and female voices are used on the tapes. There is variation in the speed of delivery of speech: within Units, Stage 1 is spoken more slowly than Stage 3, and between Units, numbers 1–4 are spoken more slowly than numbers 7–10.

HOW TO TAKE NOTES

The purpose of taking notes during a talk or a lecture is to help you concentrate on what the speaker is saying and to provide a summary for reference or revision later. The general principle in note-taking is to reduce the language by shortening sentences and words.
   The following advice and exercises will help you to take notes more efficiently and should be read and completed before trying to do the *Guided Note-taking* exercises in each Unit.

1 *Generally, if you want to take quick notes you must:*
   (a) omit completely certain sentences which are not essential to the main ideas;
   (b) concentrate on the important sentences, i.e. those which give most information, and on the important words, i.e. usually nouns, sometimes verbs or adjectives;
   (c) write in short phrases, rather than in complete sentences;
   (d) use common symbols or signs and abbreviations (see below).

2 *You can show the connections between ideas by using:*
   (a) *space*: the presentation of the notes is important—you should be able to see the main points clearly;
   (b) *numbers and letters* (as here), e.g. 1, 2, 3; (i), (ii), (iii); A, B, C; (a), (b), (c);
   (c) *underlining*, to draw attention to something or to emphasize something;
   (d) *common symbols and signs*, e.g.

∴	therefore	∵	because
✓	statement/answer is correct	×	statement/answer is wrong
?	question; is the statement correct?	/	or (this/that = this *or* that)
& or +	and/plus	—	a dash (often used to join ideas and replace words or punctuation marks that have been omitted)
,, ,,	ditto (means the same as the words immediately above the ditto marks)		
=	is/are/have/has/equals	≠	does *not* equal, differs from, is the opposite of
→	leads to/results in/causes	↛	does *not* lead to/result in/cause

3 *Abbreviations*

(a) Common general abbreviations. Many of these are to be found in an appendix in a dictionary; others are commonly used by English students. Some commonly used ones are shown below:

e.g.	for example	1st	first
i.e.	that is	2nd	second
etc.	etcetera: and so on	3rd	third etc.
cf.	compare	G.B.	Great Britain
viz.	namely	U.K.	United Kingdom
c. (or ca.)	about/approximately	Eng.	English
N.B.	note	Brit.	British
C19	nineteenth century; similarly C20 etc.	Q.	question
		A.	answer
1920s	i.e. 1920–1929; similarly 1970s etc.		

approx.	approximately	no.	number
dept.	department	p./pp.	page/pages
diff.(s)	difficult(y)(-ies)	poss.	possible/possibly
excl.	excluding	prob.	probable/probably
govt.	government	probs.	problems
imp.	important/importance	re-	with reference to/concerning
incl.	including	ref.	reference
info.	information	sts.	students
lang.	language	tho'	though
ltd.	limited	thro'	through
max.	maximum	v.	very
min.	minimum		

Note: English students often shorten words ending in '-ion' by writing 'n' instead of these letters, e.g. 'attent^n' instead of 'attention'. Similarly words ending in '-ment' are often represented by 't' for the letters, e.g. 'develop^t' for 'development'.

(b) Abbreviations of common words and phrases in an academic subject, e.g. an economist would abbreviate economics to econ., Gross National Product to G.N.P., balance of payments to b. of p. etc. These abbreviations will depend upon individual needs.

4 *Note-taking: Example and Exercise*

Imagine that what follows is the beginning of a lecture. The important information-words have been underlined and form the basis of the notes. (Each sentence is numbered in brackets.)

'(1) I'd like today to tell you something about Study Skills. (2) I want first of all to explain what's meant by this term and briefly indicate the main skills involved.'

SUGGESTED NOTES:

Study Skills

1   Explain term & indicate main skills

COMMENTS:

Sentence (1):   The only important information is the title; everything else can be omitted.

Sentence (2):   The lecturer explains the framework of the lecture—'first of all' is written as a numeral—1. Notice how *only* the information words need be written. Words like 'this' and 'the' are omitted. 'And' is written '&'.

Now you suggest notes for the third sentence below. Write in the space provided:
'(3) After that I want to go on to look in some detail at each of the study skills one by one.'

NOTES: _____

The lecture continues:
'(4) Firstly, then, what's meant by 'Study Skills'? (5) Quite simply this refers to all the skills that a student needs to develop in order to get maximum benefit from his studies. (6) All students who are going to study through the medium of English already know some English—some a lot, others relatively little. (7) A course in 'Study Skills' aims to apply this existing knowledge of English to the particular skills needed for academic purposes.'

SUGGESTED NOTES: (Notes from previous exercise in brackets)

(Study Skills)

(1   Explain term & indicate main skills.)
(2   Study skills 1 by 1.)

St. sk = skills stud. needs to get max. benefit from studies.
Course = apply knowledge of Eng. to academic purposes.

COMMENTS:

Sentence (4):   This repeats and reminds us of the theme of this first part of the lecture. The only necessary note is an abbreviation for the title—'St. sk.'

Sentence (5):   The 'equals sign' (=) is used to show that the lecturer is defining/explaining. Notice how some of the commonly used information-words are abbreviated: stud., max.; 'all the skills' is shortened to 'skills', omitting 'all the'.

Sentence (6):   This is an obvious statement; nothing needs to be noted.

Sentence (7):   'A course in Study Skills' is shortened to 'Course'. The 'equals sign' (=) is used to show what the course is, or consists of. 'English' is abbreviated to 'Eng.'.

Now suggest notes for the next part of the lecture. Write in the space provided:

'Let's now briefly mention the main "Study Skills" in question. Firstly, almost all students have to attend a large number of lectures, therefore they must be able not only to understand them but also take notes at the same time. Secondly, they must write essays, reports and sometimes dissertations or theses: the appropriate type of writing is usually very formal—what is often called "academic". Next, all students have a lot of reading to do, so much that it's important to be able to read in English as quickly and accurately as possible. Finally, students might have to attend discussions, often with

13

native-speakers of English, and they are expected to make contributions to these discussions.

'Now let's look at each of these Study Skills in turn, in greater detail. Firstly, understanding lectures and taking notes etc. etc.'

NOTES:

_____
_____
_____
_____
_____
_____
_____

SUGGESTED NOTES:

Study Skills: 1 large no. of lectures ∴ understand & take notes
(or: St. Sk.) 2 write essays etc.—writing = v. formal/academic
             3 lot of reading—quickly & accurately
             4 discussions—make contributions
(1) *Understand lectures & taking notes:* . . .

5 *Final Comments on Note-taking*
   (1) Generally, in note-taking an English student would probably abbreviate words more than in the examples shown here because he is more familiar with the language. He would also develop more of his own personal abbreviations and symbols: you can also do this as you become more familiar with note-taking. We suggest that you write the word in full the first time and abbreviate it when it is repeated.
   (2) In the *Guided Note-taking* exercises in each Unit the cue words that are included in order to help you take notes are in exactly the same order as they appear in the talk. No paraphrasing has been employed. An English student would probably make use of paraphrasing instead of writing down exactly the same words as in the talk. This, however, is a more advanced skill which could be encouraged in the *Alternative Guided Note-taking* exercises.
   (3) The *Guided Note-taking* exercises in the first few units give more help than in the last few units. Similarly, the first part of the *Alternative Guided Note-taking* exercise in Unit 1 has been completed. This gradual withdrawal of help is deliberate.

UNIT 1
SOME OF THE PROBLEMS FACING
LEARNERS OF ENGLISH

Unit 1   Stage 1   Dictation

(The Text is in the *Key to the Exercises*, at the back of the book.)

Either the tape of Stage 1 can be played, and a pause button used to give time to write on paper, or the teacher can read the Text as a dictation.

Unit 1   Stage 2
Exercise 1   Listening Comprehension

Read the following sentences and as you listen to the Stage 2 talk decide whether they are true or false *according to the passage*. Write T (true) or F (false) in the brackets ( ) after each sentence.

1   There are three types of problems: sociological, cultural and linguistic.   ( )
2   The linguistic problems are discussed in most detail.   ( )
3   In order to understand English people better, perhaps the most important thing for a student to do is to listen to the radio and TV.   ( )
4   The advice given on how to improve spoken English will seem difficult to follow.   ( )
5   A student should try to think in English *and* translate from his mother tongue.   ( )

Unit 1   Stage 2
Exercise 2   Listening and Blank-filling

Complete the following by writing *one or more words* in each space as you listen to the talk.

SOME OF THE PROBLEMS FACING LEARNERS OF ENGLISH

1 Today _____ like to talk about some of the problems that students face
2 when they follow a course of study through the medium of English—if English is
3 not their mother _____ .
4   The problems _____ divided into three broad categories: psycho-
5 logical, cultural and linguistic. The first two categories mainly affect those who come
6 to study in Britain. _____ comment only briefly on these two categories
7 and then spend most of the time looking at linguistic difficulties which apply to
8 everyone. Some _____ common psychological problems really involve
9 fear of the unknown: for example, whether one's academic _____ will
10 be too difficult. Looking at the cultural problems, we can see that some of them
11 _____ a very practical nature, _____ arranging satisfactory
12 accommodation. Others are less easy to define.
13   The largest category seems to be linguistic. _____ look at this in
14 some detail. Most students, in their own countries, _____ little oppor-
15 tunity to practise using English. When foreign learners first have the opportunity to
16 speak to an English-speaking person they may have a shock: they often have
17 great difficulty in understanding! I'll just mention three of the possible reasons
18 _____ .
19   First, it seems to students that English people speak very quickly. Second, they
20 speak with a variety _____ . Third, different styles of speech are used.
21 For all of these reasons students will have difficulty, mainly because they lack
22 everyday _____ in listening to English people speaking English.
23   What can a student do then to overcome these difficulties? Obviously, attend
24 English classes and if a _____ laboratory is available use it as much as
25 possible. He should also _____ to programmes in English on the radio
26 and TV. Perhaps most important of all, he should take every opportunity to meet
27 and speak with native English-speaking people.
28   In addition, the student probably has difficulty in speaking English _____ .
29 The advice here will seem difficult to follow but _____ necessary.
30 Firstly, he must simplify what he wants to say so _____ express himself
31 reasonably clearly. Secondly, _____ try to *think* in English, not translate
32 from his mother tongue. This'll only begin to take place when his use of English
33 becomes automatic; using a language laboratory and listening _____
34 English as possible will help.

Unit 1   Stage 2
Exercise 3   Reading Comprehension

Read the following sentences and as you read the text opposite (see Exercise 2) decide if they are true or false *according to the passage*. You must (i) write T or F in the brackets and (ii) justify your answer, in the space provided, by giving evidence (i.e. by quoting) from the talk.

1   The speaker says he will not spend a long time talking about the psychological and cultural problems.   ( )

_____

_____

_____

2   The cultural problems are all of a very practical nature.   ( )

_____

_____

_____

3   There are really only three reasons for having difficulty in understanding people.
                                                                                 ( )

_____

_____

_____

4   The speaker says that students speak with a variety of accents.   ( )

_____

_____

_____

5   Using a language laboratory helps a student to translate into English automatically.   ( )

_____

_____

_____

Unit 1   Stage 2
Exercise 4   Verb stem + *ing*
(see Stage 2 Text: Exercise 2)

The following exercises practise the form and use of the *verb stem + ing*. By *verb stem* is meant the basic form of the verb, è.g. *talk*.

(a) The construction *preposition + verb stem + ing* occurs in the talk.

| They often have great difficulty *in* understand*ing* | (line 16–17) |

Now find two more examples from the talk and write them below:

1   . . . . they _____

_____

2   . . . . the student _____

_____

(b) Complete the following conversation by writing the appropriate form of a suitable verb selected from the list below:

| express/understand/read/use/follow/tell/borrow/speak/listen/ask |

Tutor :   I know *your* English is very good, but have you had any difficulties in _____ the lectures?

Student :   Yes, a few problems in _____ the various accents.

Tutor :   Perhaps you need more practice in _____ to the different British accents, then.

Student :   That's right. And then there are the different styles of _____ .

Tutor :   You mean formal and informal: the lecturer's way of _____ himself.

Student :   Exactly. One lecturer, for example, always starts his talk by _____ a couple of jokes.

Tutor :   Ah yes. I know that man. He always insists on _____ a very informal style, with lots of slang. How do you manage in such cases?

Student :   By _____ lecture notes from the other students, and by _____ them questions on things I haven't understood. You can get a lot of help through _____ the hand-outs as well.

Unit 1   Stage 2
Exercise 5   Giving Advice: '*Should*'
(see Stage 2 Text: Exercise 2)

(a) In the talk the speaker gives advice on a number of matters. Notice *how* he does this (i.e. the construction he uses).

1   '*should*' = a firm suggestion (almost 'it is your duty to'):

> He *should* also listen to programmes in English on the radio and TV.   (line 25–26)

Now find one more example from the talk and write it below:

_____

_____

2   '*must*' = indicates necessity ('it is necessary to'):

> .... he *must* simplify what he wants to say   (line 30)

Now find one more example from the talk and write it below:

_____

_____

NOTE: *should* and *must* are often called *modal verbs* or *modals*. Other modals include: *will, shall, might, ought to, can*, etc. THEY ARE ALWAYS FOLLOWED BY THE *VERB STEM*.

(b) Give advice in the following situations by using a sentence containing *should*.
(i) Use an adverb opposite in meaning to the one used in the problem, e.g.

Problem   **Advice**

| That student speaks too quickly. | → | He *should* speak *more slowly*. |

1   He speaks too quietly when he   → _____
    talks to his tutor.   _____
2   He writes rather carelessly when   → _____
    he does his essays.   _____
3   He often arrives late for classes → _____
    and seminars.   _____

(ii) The following exercises are more difficult than those above.
    Use *should* again in giving advice, but note that the sentence construction will be more varied than in (i).

4   He never checks his written work   → _____
    for mistakes in spelling.   _____
5   He doesn't attend all the lectures → _____
    that have been recommended.   _____
6   He doesn't write up his lecture
    notes soon after the lecture has   → _____
    finished.   _____

Unit 1   Stage 3   Guided Note-taking

Complete the following as you listen to the Stage 3 talk.

Title: . . . .

Purpose: 1   aware . . . .
            2   suggest . . . .

3 categories: 1   . . . .
              2   Cultural
              3   . . . .
   1   Some = fear . . . . e.g. . . . .
. . . . Also . . . .
. . . ., poss. homesickness etc.
   2   Some = v. practical e.g. . . . .
      Brit. way of life e.g. . . . .
      . . . .
   3   Little practice. . . . .
      When 1st speak to Eng. person = ...
      Great diff. . . . .
      Reasons: (i)   Eng. people . . . .
             (ii)   ,,   ,, ... ,. .
                . . . .
             (iii)   Different styles (speech) . . . .
                . . . .

What can student do?
   (a)   . . . . & lang. lab.
   (b)   . . . .
   (c)   Most imp. = ...
Prob. diff. in . . . .
   Advice: 1   . . . .
          2   try to . . . . NOT . . . .
          3   practise . . . .
          4   . . . .

Abbreviations used above:

poss.	= possible	diff.	= difficulty
v.	= very	lang. lab.	= language laboratory
Brit.	= British	imp.	= important
1st	= first	prob.	= probable
Eng.	= English	e.g.	= for example

Unit 1 Stage 3 Alternative Guided Note-taking

Listen to the Stage 3 talk and take notes using the lecturer's signals (listed below) to help you. These can be written in the book or on a separate piece of paper. The first part has been done for you.

Lecturer's signals	Notes
Today I'd like to talk about	*Problems facing learners of English.*
The purpose is	*show aware + suggest how overcome*
The problems can be divided into	*3 categories :* ....
I'll comment only briefly on these first two and then spend most of the time looking at linguistic difficulties . . .	
Some of the common	*(1) Psychological — some = fear of unknown*
For example	*e.g. academic studies = too difficult? ...*
. . . also	*separation from family / homesickness.*
Looking now at	*(2) Cultural* ....
we can see	*some = v. practical*
e.g.	*e.g. arranging accomodation* ......
Some	*some = less easy to define* ....
. . . in other words	*i.e. British way of life* ....
Such difficulties include	*e.g. strong environ., social habits, etc.*
The largest category is	(3) ....
Let's look at this in some detail	
In other words	....
There are a number of reasons for this. I'll just mention three . . .	
Firstly	(i) ....
Secondly	(ii) ....
Thirdly	(iii) ....
e.g.	....
What can a student do then to overcome these difficulties? Well	
....	(i) ....
. . . also	(ii) ....
Perhaps most important of all ...	(iii) ....
In addition to these problems ...	(4) ....
The advice here	....
Firstly	(i) ....
. . . for example	....
Secondly	(ii) ....
In general...................	(iii) ....
. . . also	(iv) ....

21

Unit 1   Stage 3   Follow-up Activity 1*

Requesting Clarification

Sometimes, after a lecture, you will find that you were unable to note down all the points you identified as being important—in other words, there will be omissions or points of uncertainty in your notes which you will need to clarify.

Read through your notes and, using the framework below to guide you, see if the rest of the class (or your teacher) can help you complete your notes.

When		What happened	
At the beginning In the second part Towards the end	of the lecture	The lecturer	said something about . . . . mentioned . . . . gave a reference.

What didn't happen			
I'm afraid I didn't	understand catch	what	it was. s/he meant. s/he said next.

Example:
'In the third part of the lecture, the lecturer mentioned three reasons for students having difficulty in understanding. I'm afraid I didn't catch what the second one was.'

Note: In Unit 8: Stage 2: Exercise 5 you will have the opportunity for further practice in asking for clarification.

Follow-up Activity 2*

Discussion

1   Read through your notes and consider the following questions. As you do so, you may find it helpful to make one or two notes.

—Which of the categories of problems mentioned have you personally experienced? To what degree?

—Which category of problems do you anticipate facing in the future?

—The lecturer gives a number of examples of the problems discussed. Can you add any from your own experience?

—Have you tried any of the ways of overcoming the linguistic difficulties suggested by the lecturer? With what degree of success? Have you any further advice to offer your fellow students?

2   Working in groups of 3 or 4, compare your thoughts on the above.

UNIT 2
LISTENING AND UNDERSTANDING

Unit 2   Stage 1   Dictation
(The Text is in the *Key to the Exercises*, at the back of the book.)

Either the tape of Stage 1 can be played, and a pause button used to give time to write on paper, or the teacher can read the Text as a dictation.

Unit 2   Stage 2
Exercise 1   Listening Comprehension

Read the following sentences and as you listen to the Stage 2 talk decide whether they are true or false *according to the passage*. Write T (true) or F (false) in the brackets ( ) after each sentence.

1   It is as easy to identify words in speech as in print.   (   )
2   The problem of identifying weak forms and unstressed syllables only occurs in
    speech.   (   )
3   It is not difficult to remember what has been said because it can usually be heard
    more than once.   (   )
4   When students understand and remember all the words they usually follow the
    argument.   (   )
5   A more colloquial style of speech is less easy to follow than a more formal one.
                                                                                       (   )

Unit 2   Stage 2
Exercise 2   Listening and Blank-Filling

Complete the following by writing *one or more words* in each space as you listen to the talk.

LISTENING AND UNDERSTANDING

1   A student learning English _____ the following three problems when
2   _____ to talks or lectures.
3   Firstly, he _____ identify all the words correctly. I refer here to
4   known words, _____ words which the student would recognize in print.
5   Let's examine some of the reasons for this particular difficulty. In writing,
6   _____ spaces between each word. In speech, however, it's very difficult
7   to decide where one word _____ and the next one begins. In writing,
8   all the letters are easy to identify. In speech, many of the sounds cause a student
9   difficulty and he _____ to identify them. Some words in English have
10   a _____ form which non-native speakers only identify with difficulty.
11   The students also _____ find it difficult to hear the unstressed syllable
12   in a word. This problem doesn't occur in print.
13   The second main problem is the difficulty of remembering _____ said.
14   Words in print are permanently fixed in space. They can, therefore, _____
15   again and again. In speech, however, words disappear immediately after _____
16   _____ spoken. The listener has to concentrate very hard, therefore, on identifying
17   and understanding them *immediately*. _____ no chance of hearing them
18   a second time.
19   Thirdly, there's the problem of following the _____ . Students may
20   frequently have difficulty with this even when they understand and remember all
21   the words. I want to suggest three reasons _____ . Firstly, the students
22   _____ always recognize the important points. Secondly, in trying to
23   understand small points, they may miss the big ones. Thirdly, because they're
24   concentrating on taking notes, they may miss developments in the argument.
25   In addition, students have difficulty understanding different accents. Many
26   _____ will have a B.B.C.-type accent, though others will have a different
27   pronunciation. It's usually the vowels _____ pronounced differently,
28   but sometimes the consonants, too. The style of English a lecturer _____
29   may also cause problems. A more _____ style can generally be followed
30   more easily than a colloquial one.

Unit 2   Stage 2
Exercise 3   Reading Comprehension

Read the following sentences and as you read the text above (see Exercise 2) decide if they are true or false *according to the passage*. You must (i) write T or F in the brackets and (ii) justify your answer, in the space provided, by giving evidence (i.e. by quoting) from the talk.

1   In speech, as in writing, there are spaces between words.   ( )

_____

_____

_____

2   Letters in writing are easier to identify than sounds in speech.   (   )

_____

_____

_____

3   The listener must put a lot of effort into recognizing and understanding the
words as soon as they are spoken.   (   )

_____

_____

_____

4   Developments in the argument will always be noticed if students concentrate
on taking notes.   (   )

_____

_____

_____

5   Difficulty in understanding different accents is most often caused by variations
in the pronunciation of vowels.   (   )

_____

_____

_____

Unit 2   Stage 2
Exercise 4   Verb stem + *s*
(see Stage 2 Text: Exercise 2)

Students often find it difficult to identify verb endings accurately when they listen
to continuous speech. This is particularly true of the 'third person singular—s'
ending, which is also frequently omitted when lecture notes are finally written up.

(a) For each of the spaces below
(i) choose an appropriate verb (or verbal auxiliary) from the list provided.
(ii) write the appropriate form of the verb.
Use each verb only once. The first verb has been done for you. The sentences
have been adapted from the talk.

| do   finish   cause   identify   have   start   pronounce   meet |
| take   use   fail   speak   occur   arise   listen |

A student learning English occasionally (1) _____meets_____ the following
problems when he (2) _____ to talks or lectures. It is difficult to
decide where one word (3) _____ and the next one (4) _____
_____. In speech, many sounds (5) _____ a student difficulty
and he (6) _____ to identify them. Some words in English, which
(7) _____ very commonly, (8) _____ a weak form. An
overseas student only (9) _____ them with difficulty. In addition,

25

many students sometimes (10) _____ not hear the unstressed syllable in a word. This problem never (11) _____ in print.

The lecturer who (12) _____ an informal style and who (13) _____ his vowels with a strong accent will be difficult to follow. A student (14) _____ notes more easily when the lecturer (15) _____ with a B.B.C. accent.

[Check your answers before proceeding to exercise (b).]

(b) The 'third person singular—s' ending may be *pronounced* /s/, /z/ or /ɪz/ depending on the sound which precedes it. Write each of the *verb stem + s* verbs from exercise (a) above in the appropriate column of the table below. The first example has been done for you.

/s/	/z/	/ɪz/
meets		

Unit 2   Stage 2
Exercise 5   Adverbs of Frequency
(see Stage 2 Text: Exercise 2)

Adverbs of frequency (i.e. adverbs which answer the question 'how often', such as *often*, *sometimes*, *generally*, *frequently*, *rarely*, *never*) can be used to modify the action of a verb; they may be used to render a statement less definite or more cautious.

(a) They are normally placed immediately before the verb stem, e.g.

| A student learning English *often finds* the following three problems.... | (line 1) |

Now find another example from the talk where an adverb of frequency is placed in the same position:

_____

_____

(b) When the verb in a sentence has two (or more) auxiliaries before the verb stem, e.g. *can be followed*, the adverb of frequency usually comes *after* the *first* auxiliary, e.g.

| A lecture *can usually be* followed more easily if the speaker *uses* the blackboard well. | (not in the Text) |

Now find a similar example *in the Text*:

_____

_____

(c) The table below shows the more common adverbs of frequency:

never	rarely seldom	occasionally	sometimes	often frequently	usually normally generally regularly	always

Complete the passage below by adding an appropriate adverb from this table to each of the 7 verb phrases in italics.
(i) Indicate by a stroke (/) where the adverb should go and
(ii) write the adverb to the left of the vertical line. The first example has been done for you. Sometimes there may be more than one appropriate adverb. As far as possible keep to the original sense of the passage.

_____often_____ 1	In a lecture, identifying all the words correctly (1) *can/be* a serious problem. It is perhaps surprising that even the simplest words, like 'have', 'are', 'the', etc., (2) *may be misunder-*
_____ 2	
_____ 3	*stood.* A lecturer (3) *repeats* sentences so a
_____ 4	student (4) *must understand* immediately. However, even if he knows and recognizes all the vocabulary
_____ 5	it is possible that he (5) *may fail* to understand the sense. The question of accent is important too: although one cannot say that a lecturer with a B.B.C. accent (6) *causes* problems he
_____ 6	
_____ 7	(7) *will be followed* more easily than a lecturer with a marked regional accent.

Unit 2 Stage 3 Guided Note-Taking

Complete the following as you listen to the Stage 3 talk.

Title: . . . .

Probs.:

1 Doesn't identify . . . .

   Reasons: (i) in speech 1 word . . . .

              (ii) . . . . = v. diff.

                   to identify

          (iii) Some words pronounced . . . .

                  e.g. . . . .

                  . . . . e.g. <u>cotton</u>, <u>carbon</u>

2 Remembering . . . .

   In listening got to . . . .

   Concentrate on . . . .

   In for. lang. brain . . . .

   In own lang. . . . .

3 Can't follow . . . . (partly due to . . . .)

   <u>Why?</u> (1) don't recognize . . . .

           (2) try too hard to . . . .

           (3) . . . .

Other probs.:

   (a) <u>Pron.</u> of Eng. changes . . . .

        & from . . . . e.g. . . . .

        N.B. usually vowels . . . .

   (b) <u>Sty</u>le of Eng. — v. formal — or . . . .

                              . . . .

               more formal = ...

                             . . . .

   (c) <u>Also</u>: . . . .

        common use of irony

        . . . . etc.

New abbreviations used above:

diff. = difficult   pron. = pronunciation
for. = foreign   N.B. = note

Unit 2   Stage 3   Alternative Guided Note-taking

Listen to the Stage 3 talk and take notes using the lecturer's signals (listed below) to help you. These can be written in the book or on a separate piece of paper.

Lecturer's signals	Notes
(Title)	. . . .
. . . the following	. . . .
Firstly	(1) . . . .
Let's examine some of	. . . .
	(i) . . . .
	(ii) . . . .
Finally	(iii) (a) . . . .
. . . for example	. . . .
Furthermore	(b) . . . .
For instance	. . . .
But I want now to come on to the second main problem	(2) . . . .
	(i) . . . .
	(ii) . . . .
	(iii) . . . .
	(iv) . . . .
Thirdly I want to deal with a problem. The problem is this	(3) . . . .
Why is this? I'll suggest	. . . .
Firstly	(i) . . . .
Secondly	(ii) . . . .
Thirdly	(iii) . . . .
There are, however, other problems . . . I'd like to mention briefly	(4) (i) . . . .
To give an example	. . . .
It's worth noticing	. . . .
. . . also	(ii) . . . .
By . . . I mean	. . . .
Generally speaking	. . . .
Other factors, which I haven't the time to discuss in detail . . . include	(iii) . . . .
	. . . .

Unit 2   Stage 3   Follow-up Activity 1*

Oral Reconstruction and Checking/Completion of Notes

1   Working in groups of 3 or 4, each of you should take it in turn to try and reconstruct a part of the talk from your notes, using the signals in the *Alternative Guided Note-taking* exercise to help you. As you listen to each other you should mark your notes in the following way:

= : a point made by a fellow student appears in your notes.
− : a fellow student omits a point appearing in your notes.
+ : a fellow student makes a point omitted in your notes (you should, of course, also note the point made).

2   Discuss any differences noted (i.e. points omitted or additional points made by fellow students) and try to agree on a set of notes.

3   Ask the rest of the class (or the teacher) for any further clarification that may be necessary (see Unit 1: Stage 3: Follow-up Activity 1).

Follow-up Activity 2*

Writing

Use your completed notes to write a 50–75 word summary of the talk.

UNIT 3
LECTURES AND NOTE-TAKING

Unit 3   Stage 1   Dictation

(The Text is in the *Key to the Exercises*, at the back of the book.)

Either the tape of Stage 1 can be played, and a pause button used to give time to write on paper, or the teacher can read the Text as a dictation.

Unit 3   Stage 2
Exercise 1   Listening Comprehension

Read the following sentences and as you listen to the Stage 2 talk decide whether they are true or false *according to the passage*. Write T (true) or F (false) in the brackets ( ) after each sentence.

1   A student normally has only one chance to understand the lecturer.   ( )
2   You can be sure that a lecturer will always indicate if an important point is to follow.   ( )
3   A student needs to make a note of every point that the lecturer makes.   ( )
4   A student should write his notes when the lecturer is giving important information.   ( )
5   Spacing and underlining help to show the structure of the lecture.   ( )

Unit 3   Stage 2
Exercise 2   Listening and Blank-filling

Complete the following by writing *one or more words* in each space as you listen to the talk.

LECTURES AND NOTE-TAKING

1 When a student takes notes in a lecture he _____ do four things.
2   Firstly, he has to understand _____ , *as the speaker says it*. He
3 _____ stop the lecture in order to look up a new word or check an
4 unfamiliar sentence _____ .
5   The second thing the student has to do is to decide what's important in the lecture.
6 Often the lecturer signals _____ . He may do this directly or indirectly.
7 If he _____ 'This next point is important', the student will have little
8 difficulty. The lecturer may, however, use a more colloquial style. A sentence
9 _____ 'This is the crunch', meaning _____ the really im-
10 portant point, will often cause difficulty. Many lecturers pause, and speak more
11 slowly and loudly, when _____ making an important point. If the
12 student can't recognize these _____ signals, _____ find it
13 difficult to decide what's important.
14   The third task _____ the student is that he has to write down the
15 important points. There are two problems here in addition to _____
16 what's important. The first one is speed. The second one is clarity. The student
17 _____ abbreviate, should write down the important information words
18 (usually nouns, sometimes verbs or adjectives) and should write one point on each
19 line. He _____ , if possible, _____ a moment to write when
20 the lecturer _____ giving vital information.
21   Finally, the student's notes must show the connections between the various points
22 _____ noted. If he makes intelligent use of spacing and underlining,
23 together with the employment of conventional _____ and the numbering
24 of points, _____ to understand the framework of the lecture more easily.

Unit 3   Stage 2
Exercise 3   Reading Comprehension

Read the following sentences and as you read the text above (see Exercise 2) decide if they are true or false *according to the passage*. You must (i) write T or F in the brackets and (ii) justify your answer, in the space provided, by giving evidence (i.e. by quoting) from the talk.

1   It is not practical to use a dictionary during a lecture.   ( )

_____

_____

_____

2 It is helpful to students if a lecturer speaks colloquially.   ( )

_____

_____

_____

3 Pausing and speaking more clearly and loudly are direct signals of an important
point.   ( )

_____

_____

_____

4 Nouns are normally the most important type of words to include in notes. ( )

_____

_____

_____

5 If a student wishes to make the structure of a lecture clear he should organize
his note-taking so that it shows the connections between important points. ( )

_____

_____

_____

Unit 3   Stage 2
Exercise 4   Situations and Advice: Conditional Sentences

(a) Lecturers often have to say what will occur in a given situation. They frequently
employ the following type of conditional clause to convey this:

| If he says 'this next point is important', the student will have little difficulty. | (line 7–8) |

i.e. *If + subject + simple present tense, subject + will + stem.*

State what you think will occur in the following situations which have been
mentioned in the talk:
(i) If the student doesn't recognize the lecturer's indirect signals (e.g. loudness
and speed), he _____

_____

(ii) If the student spaces his notes out sensibly in numbered points, _____

_____

(b) Tutors often use the same sentence pattern when giving advice to students. The
verb in the main clause, however, is usually *must,* or *should,* or *will have to,*
depending on how emphatic the advice is and what the relationship is with the
person being spoken to.

Give helpful advice to a fellow-student by completing the following sentences. The first one has been done for you.

1 If you want to apply for a postgraduate course, <u>you should first write for an application form.</u>

2 If your conversational English is weak, you ⎯⎯⎯⎯⎯⎯⎯⎯⎯⎯⎯

⎯⎯⎯⎯⎯⎯⎯⎯⎯⎯⎯⎯⎯⎯⎯⎯⎯⎯⎯⎯⎯⎯⎯⎯⎯⎯⎯⎯

3 If you can't hear the lecture when you sit at the back of the room, ⎯⎯⎯

⎯⎯⎯⎯⎯⎯⎯⎯⎯⎯⎯⎯⎯⎯⎯⎯⎯⎯⎯⎯⎯⎯⎯⎯⎯⎯⎯⎯

4 If you need practice in listening to English, ⎯⎯⎯⎯⎯⎯⎯⎯⎯⎯⎯

⎯⎯⎯⎯⎯⎯⎯⎯⎯⎯⎯⎯⎯⎯⎯⎯⎯⎯⎯⎯⎯⎯⎯⎯⎯⎯⎯⎯

Now state the situation for which the following advice is suitable.

5 If ⎯⎯⎯⎯⎯⎯⎯⎯⎯⎯⎯⎯⎯⎯⎯⎯⎯⎯⎯⎯⎯⎯⎯⎯⎯⎯ ,
   you should ask the librarian.

6 If ⎯⎯⎯⎯⎯⎯⎯⎯⎯⎯⎯⎯⎯⎯⎯⎯⎯⎯⎯⎯⎯⎯⎯⎯⎯⎯ ,
   you will have to join some university societies.

7 If ⎯⎯⎯⎯⎯⎯⎯⎯⎯⎯⎯⎯⎯⎯⎯⎯⎯⎯⎯⎯⎯⎯⎯⎯⎯⎯ ,
   you must look at the accommodation advertisements in the local newspaper.

Unit 3   Stage 2
Exercise 5   Revision: Missing Words

Below is part of the Stage 2 Text. In each line one word has been omitted. You must (i) decide which word is missing, (ii) indicate by a stroke (/) where it should go, and (iii) write the word to the left of the vertical line. The first line has been done for you as an example.

is (or: 's)	1	Firstly, he has to understand what/said, as the
⎯⎯⎯⎯	2	speaker says it. He can't stop the lecture order
⎯⎯⎯⎯	3	to look up a new word or check unfamiliar sentence
⎯⎯⎯⎯	4	pattern. The second thing the student to do is
⎯⎯⎯⎯	5	to decide what important in the lecture. Often
⎯⎯⎯⎯	6	the lecturer signals this. He may this directly
⎯⎯⎯⎯	7	or indirectly. If he 'This next point is
⎯⎯⎯⎯	8	important', the student have little difficulty.
⎯⎯⎯⎯	9	The lecturer may, however, a more colloquial
⎯⎯⎯⎯	10	style. A sentence as 'This is the crunch',
⎯⎯⎯⎯	11	meaning this the really important point, will
⎯⎯⎯⎯	12	often difficulty. Many lecturers pause, and
⎯⎯⎯⎯	13	speak more slowly and loudly, when are making
⎯⎯⎯⎯	14	an important point. The student can't recognize
⎯⎯⎯⎯	15	these indirect signals, he'll find difficult to
		decide what's important.

Unit 3   Stage 3   Guided Note-taking

Complete the following as you listen to the Stage 3 talk.

Title: . . . .

4 most _____ :

  1 Understand what lecturer says . . . .

      cannot . . . .

      Often poss. to understand much by . . . .

      . . . .

  2 What's imp.?

      Most imp. info. = ... make sure . . . .

      . . . .

            implies . . . .

        Good lecturer . . . .

      . . . . or . . . . signals

          Explicit = write it down!

          Indirect = ... or . . . . etc.

              = sth. imp.

              . . . .

              . . . .

              = sth. incidental

  3 Main points: write them down — has to do . . . .

      . . . .

        (i) helps to . . . .

        (ii) select only words → . . . . = ...

        (iii) writing only . . . .

      Diff. in . . . .

      . . . . may guide:

        (a) in same direction = ...

                 e.g. . . . .

        (b) 'however' etc. = ...

  4 Show _____

      . . . . presentation:

      e.g. use of . . . . etc.

      points should . . . .

New abbreviations used above:
info. = information
sth. = something

Unit 3   Stage 3   Alternative Guided Note-taking

Listen to the Stage 3 talk and take notes using the lecturer's signals (listed below) to help you. These can be written in the book or on a separate piece of paper.

Lecturer's signals	Notes
Today I'm going to analyse	....
Firstly	(1) ....
	....
	....
	....
	....
But how does the student decide what's important?... It is, in fact, the second of the four skills I want to talk about today	(2) ....
	....
	....
...for example	....
	....
It's worth remembering that... also	....
	....
	....
...however...This is, in fact, the third basic skill.............	(3) ....
	(i) ....
...also	(ii) ....
...also	(iii) ....
An important difficulty is	(iv) ....
...are examples of this	....
...such as.......................	....
The fourth skill	(4) ....
Thus	....
...too...........................	....

Unit 3 Stage 3 Follow-up Activity 1

Comprehension Check

1 Use your notes to answer the following questions.

   (i) Which four skills does the lecturer consider to be of greatest importance in note-taking?

_____

_____

_____

_____

  (ii) What advice is given for dealing with unfamiliar words in a lecture?

_____

 (iii) Why does the lecturer suggest that unfamiliar words need not be a source of difficulty when listening to a lecture?

_____

_____

  (iv) The lecturer draws a distinction between the use of direct and indirect signals. Explain with examples.

_____

_____

_____

_____

_____

_____

_____

  (v) Why is it important to pay particular attention to connectives when listening to a lecture? Give examples.

_____

_____

_____

_____

_____

  (vi) What suggestions are made for showing the connections between points?

_____

_____

2   Compare answers with a fellow student.

3   Ask the rest of the class (or the teacher) for any further clarification that may be necessary (see Unit 1: Stage 3: Follow-up Activity 1).

Follow-up Activity 2

Review of the Lecturer's Signals
You now have some experience of the signals used by lecturers to facilitate the task of the listener. You will, therefore, have noticed that these signals convey different messages to the listener.

1   Below are some of the common messages they convey. Review the signals listed in Units 1–3 and find examples of signals conveying the following messages. Write your examples in the spaces provided. Indicate, in brackets, the number of the unit from which each example is taken.

   (i) The subject of my talk is . . .

   (ii) The scope of my discussion here will be as follows.

   (iii) The next point is under the same heading.

   (iv) The next part of my talk will be about . . .

   (v) I am now going to give/have just given you an example of the point I have just made.

   (vi) The next/last point is important.

   (vii) I am now going to explain the same point in a different way.

2   Compare examples with a fellow student and/or the teacher.

3   As you complete the remaining units add any further examples you find to the above lists. You will probably need to use a notebook.

UNIT 4
ATTITUDES TOWARDS THE LEARNING
OF VOCABULARY

Unit 4   Stage 1   Dictation
(The Text is in the *Key to the Exercises*, at the back of the book.)

Either the tape of Stage 1 can be played, and a pause button used to give time to write on paper, or the teacher can read the Text as a dictation.

Unit 4   Stage 2
Exercise 1   Listening Comprehension

Read the following sentences and as you listen to the Stage 2 talk decide whether they are true or false *according to the passage*. Write T (true) or F (false) in the brackets ( ) after each sentence.

1   There has recently been an investigation into the attitudes of undergraduate science students towards language learning.   ( )
2   An English dictionary shows that nearly all words have only one meaning. ( )
3   The use of vocabulary lists may encourage a student to think that nearly every word in English has just one meaning.   ( )
4   Every word in English has an exact translational equivalent in the student's native language.   ( )
5   To use words correctly it is not enough to learn only their meanings.   ( )

Unit 4   Stage 2
Exercise 2   Listening and Blank-filling

Complete the following by writing *one or more words* in each space as you listen to the talk.

ATTITUDES TOWARDS THE LEARNING OF VOCABULARY

1   A recent university _____ project investigated the attitudes of post-
2   graduate science students _____ the learning of English vocabulary. The
3   results were surprising. _____ three of them.
4   Firstly, most of the students think that nearly every word in English _____
5   just one meaning. This is, of course, completely contrary to the facts. A glance at
6   any English dictionary will show this. The student will frequently find seven or eight
7   meanings listed _____ 'simple' words.
8   Why, then, have _____ students made such a mistake? One reason
9   may be _____ all *science* students. Scientists try to use words in
10 _____ special subject which have one meaning, and one meaning only.
11 Another reason, of course, could be the way in which these students _____.
12 They may have used vocabulary lists when they first _____ English.
13 On one side of the page is the word in English; on the other side, a single word in
14 the student's native language.
15   The second attitude that _____ from the findings is equally mistaken.
16 Practically all the students think that every word in English has an exact translational
17 equivalent. Again, this is far from the truth. Sometimes *one word* in English can
18 only be translated by a *phrase* in the student's native language. There are _____
19 _____ difficulties in translation which we _____ mention here.
20 Certainly the idea of a one word for one word translation process is completely
21 false. Translation machines, which tried to work on this _____, failed
22 completely.
23   The third result of the investigation showed _____ error in the
24 students' thinking. They believe that as soon as they know the meaning of a word,
25 they're in a position to use it correctly. This is _____ for any language
26 but is perhaps particularly false for English. The student has to learn when to use
27 a word _____ to know what it means. Some words in English mean
28 almost the same but they can only _____ in certain situations.
29   What, then, is the best way to increase _____ vocabulary? This can
30 be answered in three words—observation, imitation and _____ .

Unit 4   Stage 2
Exercise 3   Reading Comprehension

Read the following sentences and as you read the text above (see Exercise 2) decide if they are true or false *according to the passage.* You must (i) write T or F in the brackets and (ii) justify your answer, in the space provided, by giving evidence (i.e. by quoting) from the talk.

1   Students' attitudes towards vocabulary learning, as shown in a recent investigation, were predictable.   ( )

_____

_____

_____

2   The only reason the students think that each word in English has just one meaning is because they're all science students.   ( )

_____

_____

_____

3   One word in English can usually only be translated by a phrase in other languages.   ( )

_____

_____

_____

4   Translation machines failed because they worked on the principle of a one word for one word translation process.   ( )

_____

_____

_____

5   Vocabulary lists, containing English words with a single word translation in the student's mother tongue, are the best way to increase vocabulary.   ( )

_____

_____

_____

Unit 4   Stage 2
Exercise 4   Degrees of Being Definite

(a) In academic English, words such as 'wrong', 'not correct' and 'incorrect' are often only used when a clear, factual mistake has been made (e.g. with a figure or quotation). In most other cases, alternative expressions convey a similar meaning, e.g.

.... completely contrary to the facts.	(line 5)
.... equally mistaken.	(line 15)

Now find 5 more examples from the Stage 2 talk of the speaker expressing the opinion that something is *incorrect*:

1 _____

2 _____

3 _____

4 _____

5 _____

(b) In academic English it is often necessary to indicate 'less than one hundred per cent certainty', i.e. it is necessary to be 'tentative'. The table below illustrates some of the ways in which such caution can be expressed.

BASIC MEANING		Method of expressing basic meaning			
		1	through the verb phrase	2	through the adverb
A	not definitely *true*		appears to seems to		apparently seemingly
B	not definitely *certain*		tends to (is) likely to may well		(very) probably
C	possible		may can		maybe perhaps possibly

Now modify the sentences below: refer to the table and select the appropriate method (e.g. B1, A1 etc.). The first example has been done for you.

(i) DEFINITE: Students *translate* from their first language when they write in a foreign language.

LESS DEFINITE: (B1) Students *are likely to* translate from their first language when they write in a foreign language.

(ii) DEFINITE: It's best for a student to concentrate on developing his ability.

LESS DEFINITE: (B2) _____

_____

(iii) DEFINITE: A student who studies abroad suffers from homesickness in the early stages.

LESS DEFINITE: (C1) _____

_____

(iv) DEFINITE: English people speak very quickly.

LESS DEFINITE: (A1) _____

_____

(v) DEFINITE: Watching TV is the activity that will help to develop listening comprehension the most.

LESS DEFINITE: (C2) _____

_____

Unit 4   Stage 2
Exercise 5   Vocabulary: Multiple Meaning

(a) The following words, taken from the Stage 2 Text, have several meanings listed
in the dictionary. Select the meaning which is appropriate for the text by putting
a tick in the relevant box. ☑

1 **glance** (line 5): *n.*
   1 quick turning of the eyes: *loving ~ s.* ☐
   2 quick look: *take a ~ at the newspaper
      headlines* ☐
   3 (sudden movement producing a) flash
      of light: *a ~ of spears in the sunlight* ☐

2 **then** (line 8): *adv.*
   1 at the time: *I was still unmarried ~.* ☐
   2 next; after that: *We had a week in Rome
      and ~ went to Naples.* ☐
   3 in that case; that being so: *A: 'It isn't
      here.' B: 'It must be in the next room, ~.'* ☐

3 **emerge** (line 15): *vi.*
   1 come into view; (esp.) come out (from
      water, etc.): *The moon ~ d from behind
      the clouds.* ☐
   2 (of facts, ideas) appear; become known:
      No new ideas ~ d during the talks. ☐
   3 issue (from state of suffering etc.) ☐

4 **practically** (line 16): *adv.*
   1 in a practical (as opposed to theoretical)
      manner. ☐
   2 in effect; in action: *~, his ideas did not
      work very well.* ☐
   3 almost; nearly: *He says it is ~ finished.* ☐

5 **principle** (line 21): *n.[c.]*
   1 general law shown in the working of a
      machine. ☐
   2 basic truth; general law of cause and
      effect. ☐
   3 guiding rule for behaviour: *live up to
      one's ~ s.* ☐

(b) What do the abbreviations used above mean?

   n. _____   *adv.* _____

   vi. _____   *[c.]* _____

43

Unit 4   Stage 3   Guided Note-taking

Complete the following as you listen to the Stage 3 talk.

Title: . . . .
   Univ. research: surprising . . . .

Misconceptions:

1   Every Eng. word = ...
   Majority = ...
   How arrived at false conclusion?
      (i) . . . .
      (ii) . . . .

2   Every word in Eng. = ...
                     . . . . .NO!
   S'times no equivalent: may employ . . . .
   1 word in st's. lang. = ...
                     e.g.. . . . .
   Translation = ...
           can't be done . . . .
                     . . . .

3   Word can be used correctly . . . .
                     . . . . .NO!
   Eng. = ...
           e.g. starts, & . . . . (=formal)
   More imp. = ...
           e.g.. . . . .

Best way to . . . . :
      (1) . . . .
      (2) . . . .
      (3) . . . .

New abbreviations used above:

univ.   = university   st's = student's
s'times = sometimes

Unit 4   Stage 3   Alternative Guided Note-taking

Listen to the Stage 3 talk and take notes using the lecturer's signals (listed below) to help you. These can be written in the book or on a separate piece of paper.

Lecturer's signals	Notes
(Title)	. . . .
Among the many . . . . the following . . . the most serious.	. . . .
Firstly	(1) . . . .
One wonders how, then, these students have arrived at such a false conclusion. One reason	(i) . . . .
Another reason	(ii) . . . .
But this brings me on to the second major misconception	(2) . . . .
The third important misconception	(3) . . . .
This is, of course, ...	. . . .
Perhaps more important is	. . . .
A simple example will illustrate this	. . . .
What, then, is the best way to increase one's vocabularly in a foreign language? This can be answered in three words.	
Firstly	(1) . . . .
Secondly	(2) . . . .
Finally	(3) . . . .

Unit 4   Stage 3   Follow-up Activity 1*

Requesting Clarification

Read through your notes and see if the rest of the class (or your teacher) can help you with any clarification that may be necessary.

(See Unit 1: Stage 3: Follow-up Activity 1.)

Follow-up Activity 2*

Discussion

Read through your notes and consider the following questions. As you do so, you may find it helpful to make one or two notes.

—Before the talk, did you share any of the misconceptions found to exist among the non-native English-speaking postgraduate science students questioned? If so, which?

—The lecturer offers two possible reasons for the first misconception. Which in your experience/opinion is the more likely? Give reasons.

—Can you think of any words in your first language which illustrate the problematic nature of translation?

—The lecturer suggests three ways of increasing one's vocabulary in a foreign language. Have you developed any additional strategies which you could recommend to your fellow students?

Follow-up Activity 3*

Dictionary Task

You will need both a bilingual and a monolingual English dictionary for this task.

1   Look up, in your bilingual dictionary, a word in your first language for which you do not know the English translation (you should, of course, have in mind a particular context).

2   Note down the English translations offered.

3   Look these up in a monolingual English dictionary and, using the example sentences to help you, decide which is the best English translation for the context you had in mind.

UNIT 5
EFFECTIVE READING

Unit 5   Stage 1   Dictation

(The Text is in the *Key to the Exercises*, at the back of the book.)

Either the tape of Stage 1 can be played, and a pause button used to give time to write on paper, or the teacher can read the Text as a dictation.

Unit 5   Stage 2
Exercise 1   Listening Comprehension

Read the following sentences and as you listen to the Stage 2 talk decide whether they are true or false *according to the passage*. Write T (true) or F (false) in the brackets ( ) after each sentence.

1   If students read a book slowly and carefully they usually get an overall view of the whole book.   ( )
2   Students can make their reading more effective by deciding why and what they're going to read.   ( )
3   An overview of the contents of a book can be obtained by reading the index.
                                                                              ( )
4   The only advantage of a student making notes as he reads is that they provide him with a summary.   ( )
5   A student should read as carefully as possible because he has a lot to read in a short time.   ( )

47

Unit 5   Stage 2
Exercise 2   Listening and Blank-filling

Complete the following by writing *one or more words* in each space as you listen to the talk.

EFFECTIVE READING

1 When a teacher _____ a student to read a book it's usually for a particular
2 purpose. The book may contain useful information or it may be _____
3 for the ideas that it puts forward etc. The teacher may just _____ a few
4 pages and not the whole book.
5   Unfortunately, when many students pick up a book to read *they* _____
6 have no particular purpose in mind. Often they open the book and start reading,
7 slowly and in great detail. The result is that students frequently _____
8 an overall view of what _____ reading.
9   Students can make their reading _____ effective by adopting a plan
10 aimed at helping them to understand and to remember what they read. Firstly, they
11 should decide precisely *why* they're reading the book: perhaps _____
12 understand a difficult idea or argument. Then they should decide _____
13 *what* they're going to read: a chapter of a book, for example.
14   It's helpful to get an overview of the contents before starting to read. _____
15 _____ done by reading the introduction and the conclusion, and possibly
16 skimming (or reading very quickly) some sections _____ get a general
17 idea of the contents.
18   Finally, students should ask themselves a specific question about _____
19 reading. They should then try to answer it by making notes as they read. This
20 will help _____ focus on the purpose of the reading as well as providing
21 a summary which _____ again later. This is, perhaps, _____
22 effective part of the reading strategy.
23   If a student puts into practice everything _____ suggested so far, can
24 we say that he reads efficiently? Well, we _____ remember that most
25 students have a lot to read and only a limited time in which to read it. As a result,
26 it's important that a student reads _____ quickly as possible. He should
27 aim to improve _____ his slowest speed, which is for _____
28 study, and his fastest (or skimming), which is for getting a general idea.

Unit 5   Stage 2
Exercise 3   Reading Comprehension

Read the following sentences and as you read the text above (see Exercise 2) decide if they are true or false *according to the passage.* You must (i) write T or F in the brackets and (ii) justify your answer, in the space provided, by giving evidence (i.e. by quoting) from the talk.

1   When a teacher recommends a book he never recommends the whole book. (   )

_____
_____
_____

2 It's an advantage for a student to have a particular purpose in mind when he
   starts reading.   (   )

   _____

   _____

   _____

3 The most effective part of the reading strategy is for students to answer a specific
   question that their teacher has asked.   (   )

   _____

   _____

   _____

4 For a student to read efficiently it is necessary for him to adopt the proposed
   reading strategy and read as quickly as possible.   (   )

   _____

   _____

   _____

5 A student's slowest reading speed is used for obtaining a general idea of the
   reading material.   (   )

   _____

   _____

   _____

Unit 5   Stage 2
Exercise 4   Comparisons

In the talk there are several examples of comparisons (notably lines 9, 21, 27, 28).
Comparison may be expressed either by the endings *-er* and *-est* (for adjectives and
adverbs **with one or two syllables**) or by the words *more* and *most* (if the adjective/
adverb has more than two syllables, and sometimes only two):

	WITH:	ADJ/ADV	COMPARATIVE	SUPERLATIVE
ADJECTIVES	1 or 2 syllables	easy	easier	easiest
	2/3 or more syllables	effective	more effective	most effective
ADVERBS	1 or 2 syllables	soon	sooner	soonest
	2/3 or more syllables	easily	more easily	most easily

(a) **Comparative: Adjectives/Adverbs with one or two syllables**
     Note the use of *than* after the comparative in the following example:

49

> This book is *easier* (to understand) *than* that one.

Complete the following sentences in the same way using appropriate comparatives.

1   Dr. Smith has a _____ voice _____ the other lecturer.
2   An undergraduate student works at a _____ level _____ a postgraduate student.
3   Extensive reading is normally done at a _____ speed _____ _____ intensive reading.
4   Dr. Green is getting on with his research _____ Mr. Jones.

(b) **Comparative: Adjectives/Adverbs with more than two syllables** (and sometimes only two) (i.e. +*more*)
Complete the following sentences by adding a comparative adjective or adverb, as appropriate, from the following list: *seriously, difficult, serious, practical*.

1   Dr. Anderson is _____ to understand _____ Mr. White.
2   A course in engineering has a _____ content _____ a course in philosophy.
3   The problems as regards nuclear energy are _____ we first thought.
4   The news is presented _____ in 'The Times' _____ in popular newspapers.

(c) A common way of showing that A equals B is to use the construction: *as + adjective/adverb + as*,

e.g. | Tom reads *as quickly as* John.

The negative construction is: *not + as/so + adj./adv. + as*.
    Write sentences of your own based on the following lecture notes; decide whether or not the sentences should be negative.

e.g. reading in English—difficult—speaking.

→ | Reading in English is not as difficult as speaking.

1   B.A. degree—specialized—M.A.

    _____

2   arts degree course—long—medical degree course

    _____

3   student's health—important—academic ability

    _____

4   multiple-choice questions—difficult—essay-type questions

    _____

Unit 5   Stage 2
Exercise 5   Comment Adverbials

A speaker often wishes to *comment* on the content of what he is saying. This is often done by means of sentence adverbials placed at the beginning of a sentence, e.g.

Unfortunately, when many students pick up a book to read they tend to have no particular purpose in mind.	(line 5–6)

(a) In the sentences below the *comment adverb* is underlined. Choose the appropriate part of the sentence to follow it by placing a tick in the relevant box: ☑

1   Tom studied very hard.
    <u>Surprisingly,</u>
    a he passed his exams.
    b he was not lazy.
    c he failed his exams.

2   John was late for the appointment.
    <u>Fortunately,</u>
    a he had forgotten the time.
    b his tutor was still waiting.
    c his tutor was very angry.

3   His application arrived too late.
    <u>Officially,</u>
    a it could not be accepted.
    b it did not matter.
    c it could be considered.

4   His experiment contained a few minor errors.
    <u>Basically, however,</u>
    a it was unreliable.
    b it was reliable.
    c it was inaccurate.

(b) From the following list select appropriate *comment adverbs* and write them in the spaces in the sentences: *Actually, Admittedly, Naturally, Superficially, Theoretically.*

1   _____ , the experiment had started late; but even taking this into consideration, very little had been achieved.
2   _____ , the idea was fool-proof; in practice, however, it would not work.
3   _____ , having been offered the scholarship, he accepted it at once.
4   _____ , the analysis was attractive; when examined in depth, however, it left much unexplained.
5   _____ , the idea had been first thought of in the last century, even though he claimed it was a new one.

Unit 5   Stage 3   Guided Note-taking

Complete the following as you listen to the Stage 3 talk. (NOTE: Complete the spaces in the *table* at the end of the notes with the *figures* and *percentages* given at the end of the talk.)

Title: . . . .

    When lecturer recommends book = for . . . .

      not . . . . —just . . . .

    When sts. read = ...

    Sts. often read . . . .

    <u>Result</u> = (1) no . . . .

              (2) . . . .

<u>Reading strategy</u>:

    1   Decide. . . . .

    2   ,, ...

          Starting point = ...

                 . . . .

    3   Overview of contents: reading. . . . .

                 . . . .

          Useful to. . . . .

                 . . . .

    4   Ask selves . . . . then A. it . . . .

                 . . . . : will help them to

                 . . . .

                 . . . .

               = <u>most</u> _____

         e.g. Teaching & . . . .

                 . . . .

          — Ruth Beard, ...

                 . . . .

<u>Increase reading speed</u> . . . .

    3 _____ :

        (i) . . . .

       (ii) . . . .

      (iii) . . . .

Survey — Reading Speeds (— Edward Fry):

Type of reader	Type of reading speed	Speed: words per minute (wpm)	Comprehension per cent (%)
A good reader	Skimming (v. fast)		
	Average		
	Slow/Study		
A poor reader	Skimming	—	—
	Average		
	Slow/Study		

Aim at: c. . . . .

New abbreviations used above:

A. = answer

c. = about

Unit 5   Stage 3   Alternative Guided Note-taking

Listen to the Stage 3 talk and take notes using the lecturer's signals (listed below) to help you. These can be written in the book or on a separate piece of paper.

Lecturer's signals	Notes
(Title)	. . . .
	(1) . . . .
	. . . .
Unfortunately	. . . .
	. . . .
	(2) . . . .
Firstly	(i) . . . .
Then	(ii) . . . .
. . . then	(iii) . . . .
	(a) . . . .
In addition	(b) . . . .
As well as doing this	(c) . . . .
Finally	(iv) (a) . . . .
. . . then	(b) . . . .
The importance of this last point can be seen from	. . . .
. . . it's important that	(3) . . . .
Basically, there are three main kinds of	. . . .
	(i) . . . .
. . . next is	(ii) . . . .
	(iii) . . . .
Various	. . . .
One . . . showed that	. . . .

(Use table on p.00 for remainder of note-taking.)

Note: For (1) and (2) above you will have to provide your own headings since the lecturer does not signal these.

Unit 5   Stage 3   Follow-up Activity 1*

Oral Reconstruction and Checking/Completion of Notes
See Unit 2: Stage 3: Follow-up Activity 1 for procedure.

Follow-up Activity 2*

Writing
Use your completed notes to write a 100–150 word summary of the talk.

UNIT 6
USING A LIBRARY

Unit 6   Stage 1   Dictation

(The Text is in the *Key to the Exercises*, at the back of the book.)

Either the tape of Stage 1 can be played, and a pause button used to give time to write on paper, or the teacher can read the Text as a dictation.

Unit 6   Stage 2
Exercise 1   Listening Comprehension

Read the following sentences and as you listen to the Stage 2 talk decide whether they are true or false *according to the passage*. Write T (true) or F (false) in the brackets ( ) after each sentence.

1 The main aim of the lecture is to show how a student can borrow a book more easily.   ( )
2 If a student wants to borrow a specific book, he first has to find the card for it in the name catalogue.   ( )
3 Rare books are examples of books which are to be found in the reference section of the library.   ( )
4 Reference materials can be borrowed by a student who is doing original work or research.   ( )
5 A student may often come to a library for social as well as academic reasons.
                                                                          ( )

Unit 6   Stage 2
Exercise 2   Listening and Blank-filling

Complete the following by writing *one or more words* in each space as you listen to the talk.

USING A LIBRARY

1   A student may use a library in _____ ways. First, he may borrow books
2   from it. Secondly, he may consult reference materials from its _____ .
3   Thirdly, he may use the library for general study purposes. In this lecture we shall
4   examine aspects of these activities with _____ helping the student to use
5   his library more easily and more efficiently.
6   First, then, _____ a look at how books are borrowed. Assuming the
7   student already _____ the author and title of the book he wants to
8   borrow, his first job is to consult the name _____ . This consists of a
9   list of books entered on cards. These cards are placed in alphabetical order under
10   the name of the author, institution, or editor by which the book is best _____
11   _____ . The card, apart from the author's name, always gives *at least* two other
12   important _____ information: the book's call number and its title. The
13   call number is the piece of information that enables the student to locate the book.
14   It normally _____ of two parts: the first part, or the *class* number,
15   _____ on the *top* line, tells you in what *subject area* the book _____
16   _____ ; the second part, or the author number, on the *next* line, gives the number
17   relevant to that specific author and that particular book. _____ , while
18   the class number tells the student which general _____ in the library to
19   go to in order to find the book, the author number will direct him to the exact shelf.
20   But now let's move on to reference materials. Under this heading, we usually
21   include such books as dictionaries or _____—in other words books
22   which give separate items or pieces of information _____ an account of
23   one particular subject. Again, books which are _____ or difficult to
24   replace also tend to come into this category. Finally, professional journals or
25   periodicals are usually kept in the reference section. _____ materials, of
26   course, have to remain in the library and cannot be borrowed. A student who is
27   doing original work, or research, is likely to make considerable use of such works.
28   On many _____ , however, the student may well bring with him all
29   the papers and books that he needs. He _____ to the library because
30   it provides a good study _____ and because it's a place where he can
31   easily meet and talk to his fellow students.

Unit 6   Stage 2
Exercise 3   Reading Comprehension

Read the following sentences and as you read the text opposite (see Exercise 2) decide if they are true or false *according to the passage*. You must (i) write T or F in the brackets and (ii) justify your answer, in the space provided, by giving evidence (i.e. by quoting) from the talk.

1   A student uses a library for two purposes: to borrow or consult the books and materials there.   (   )

_____

_____

_____

2   The card in the name catalogue gives a minimum of three pieces of information.   (   )

_____

_____

_____

3   The call number consists of two sets of numbers listed one above the other. (   )

_____

_____

_____

4   The author number directs a student to that section of the library where he will find the book.   (   )

_____

_____

_____

5   A periodical such as the *Journal of Linguistics* will normally be found in the lending part of the library.

_____

_____

_____

Unit 6   Stage 2
Exercise 4   Introducing Subjects

(a) The table below analyses how the speaker has introduced his subject in the Stage 2 talk. Complete the blanks with relevant parts from the Stage 2 Text. The first part has been done for you.

Speaker's aims	Language he uses
(i) To give a general introduction to the whole subject.	A student may use a library in various ways. (line 1)
(ii) To make this general introduction more specific by giving important examples.	
(iii) To explain: (a) how these examples will be treated. (b) the purpose of dealing with these examples in this way.	

(b) Now, employing the same aims as above, write *two* similar opening paragraphs (based on the information given in the table below) which will advise students how to improve their English.

	Learning device	Possible uses:		
		1st	2nd	3rd
1	Tape-recorder	improve his listening	practise speaking	record lectures
2	Dictionary	meaning of new words	spelling	how a word is used

NOTE: Although the structure of the paragraph in (a) is to be followed, small changes will be necessary in grammar and vocabulary.

1 A student _____ tape-recorder _____
_____ ways. First, he may use it to _____
_____ .
Secondly, _____ .
Thirdly, _____ .
In this talk, we shall _____
_____ with a view to _____
_____
_____ .

2 Now write the second paragraph on separate paper.

Unit 6   Stage 2
Exercise 5   Revision: Missing Words

In each line below one word has been deliberately omitted. You must (i) decide which word is missing; (ii) indicate by a stroke (/) where it should go; (iii) write the word to the left of the vertical line.

The first word has been done for you.

_____is_____	1	It/important for students to employ good study
_____	2	methods. They can, example, make their read-
_____	3	ing much effective by adopting an intelligent
_____	4	strategy. This will them to understand more
_____	5	fully and remember easily what they read. As
_____	6	well an overall strategy for reading, however,
_____	7	a student needs develop a method for building
_____	8	up large vocabulary. Many students think that
_____	9	the most effective way doing this is through
_____	10	the use of word lists. Such idea is completely
_____	11	contrary the facts. Vocabulary is best learned
_____	12	as a process of observation, imitation repetition
_____	13	in context of a student's everyday reading.
_____	14	However, still remains a further basic skill
_____	15	to be acquired, if the reader to be successful.
_____	16	He must able to use a library. In particular,
_____	17	a student who doing original work, or research,
_____	18	is likely make considerable use of the reference
_____	19	section. This contains, course, encyclopedias,
_____	20	bibliographies and professional. A student
_____	21	must know to consult these or his work will suffer.

Unit 6   Stage 3   Guided Note-taking

Complete the following as you listen to the Stage 3 talk. (NOTE: Early in the talk a *handout* and *sample card* are referred to. The sample card has been reproduced below. Label the parts of the card in the spaces provided when you hear the parts mentioned.)

Title: . . . .

3 headings: 1   . . . .

              2   . . . .

              3   . . . .

  1   Assume . . . .
        — to borrow from lib.
        — have to . . . .

Sample Card:

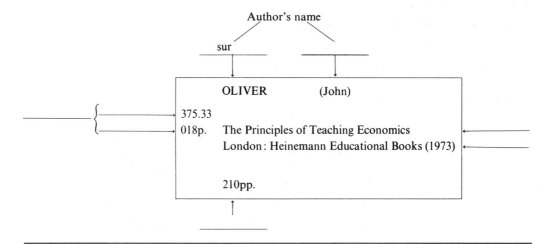

  2   Ref. section — 3 imp. types of mats.:
       (i) . . . . e.g. . . . .
      (ii) . . . . e.g. . . . .
    (iii) . . . .
    Encyclopedia gives . . . .
    Dissert./research: need to consult . . . .
                 . . . .
       v. recent research — . . . .

  3   Lib. provides . . . .
    Also chat with . . . .
    Wise to . . . .
    Q. of . . . .

New abbreviations used above:

lib. = library   mats.   = materials
ref. = reference   Dissert. = dissertation

Unit 6   Stage 3   Alternative Guided Note-taking

Listen to the Stage 3 talk and take notes using the lecturer's signals (listed below) to help you. These can be written in the book or on a separate piece of paper.

Lecturer's signals	Notes
...may be summarized under three broad headings	. . . .
	(1) . . . .
	(2) . . . .
	(3) . . . .
In this lecture we shall examine various aspects of these activities with a view to	. . . .
First of all then	(1) . . . .
Let's assume	. . . .
If you look at your hand-out	

Sample Card:

Author's name

sur

OLIVER   (John)

375.33
018p.   The Principles of Teaching Economics
         London : Heinemann Educational Books (1973)

210pp.

But now let's look at the second broad use	(2) . . . .
Three important types of materials in this section are	(i) . . . .
Examples of such . . . include	. . . .
	(ii) . . . .
An example would be	. . . .
	(iii) . . . .
. . . however	(3) . . . .
Moreover	. . . .
. . . also	. . . .
The last point, of course, is often an important one	. . . .

Unit 6   Stage 3   Follow-up Activity 1

Comprehension Check

1   Use your notes to answer the following questions.

   (i)   Each library book is identified by a call number, consisting of two parts. What are they and how do they help the student?

      (a) _____

      (b) _____

  (ii)   What are

      (a)   the imprint details?

      _____

      (b)   the collation details?

      _____

 (iii)   What type of reference does the lecturer suggest that students should consult when they are:

      (a)   starting on a new topic?

      _____

      (b)   writing a dissertation or doing a piece of research?

      _____

      (c)   interested in very recent research?

      _____

 (iv)   Why does the lecturer recommend the setting of daily targets as regards work, especially when using the library?

      _____

      _____

2   Compare answers with a fellow student.

3   Ask the rest of the class (or the teacher) for any further clarification that may be necessary (see Unit 1: Stage 3: Follow-up Activity 1).

Follow-up Activity 2*

Library Task

This is intended primarily for those students who are following the *Listening Comprehension and Note-taking Course* in an English-speaking country prior to undertaking a tertiary-level course of study or research. They will, therefore, have access to the library they will be using (or one similar) for their studies/research.

1   Find *two* references in your subject area which are kept in the university/college library to which you have access.

2   Note down the call numbers.

3   Find out where they are located.

4   Check whether they are on the shelves.

UNIT 7
PROBLEMS OF WRITING
IN A FOREIGN LANGUAGE

Unit 7   Stage 1   Dictation

(The Text is in the *Key to the Exercises*, at the back of the book.)

Either the tape of Stage 1 can be played, and a pause button used to give time to write on paper, or the teacher can read the Text as a dictation.

Unit 7   Stage 2
Exercise 1   Listening Comprehension

Read the following sentences and as you listen to the Stage 2 talk decide whether they are true or false *according to the passage*. Write T (true) or F (false) in the brackets ( ) after each sentence.

1   The learner of English finds that writing is one of the most difficult language skills.   ( )
2   The three main types of error in writing are of more or less equal importance.
                                                                                                  ( )
3   Word by word translation often results in un-English sentences.   ( )
4   Ungrammatical English always interferes with the meaning conveyed to the reader.   ( )
5   The use of a word such as 'terrific' in academic writing is an example of an error in style and usage.   ( )

Unit 7   Stage 2
Exercise 2   Listening and Blank-filling

Complete the following by writing *one or more words* in each space as you listen to the talk.

PROBLEMS OF WRITING IN A FOREIGN LANGUAGE

1 Learners of English usually find that writing is the most difficult skill they have
2 _____ . Even native-speakers of English often find it difficult to write
3 well on their special subject. It may, therefore, be helpful to _____ the
4 types of error that the learner of English usually makes. Three broad types can be
5 distinguished. _____ be discussed in order of importance.
6   The first type of error is the error _____ to a misunderstanding or,
7 even worse, to a breakdown in communication. The causes _____
8 misunderstandings and breakdowns are _____ . We can only try to
9 cover the most important here. Firstly, the student _____ to work out
10 a sentence in his own language and then tries to translate it word by word into
11 English. _____ often produces non-English sentence _____ .
12 Secondly, the student may confuse grammatical patterns _____ similar
13 in form but very different in meaning. Thirdly, he may _____ to write
14 sentences which are too long and _____ instead of simpler ones which
15 he can handle more easily. Finally, he may produce a phrase _____ a
16 sentence, with the result that the reader doesn't know what it _____ .
17   The second type of error is the error which leads to ungrammatical English, but
18 which doesn't usually _____ with the meaning. The wrong selection of
19 a verb tense often _____ this category. Other mistakes which feature
20 prominently here are really slips. If the student _____ his work carefully,
21 he can correct them himself. When he writes, therefore, he should prepare several
22 drafts.
23   The third type of error _____ style and usage. When a student writes
24 'The results of the research were terrific', _____ making this type of
25 mistake. Native speakers of English would understand but, of course, _____
26 never use the word 'terrific' in their own academic writing.

Unit 7   Stage 2
Exercise 3   Reading Comprehension

Read the following sentences and as you read the text above (see Exercise 2) decide if they are true or false *according to the passage*. You must (i) write T or F in the brackets and (ii) justify your answer, in the space provided, by giving evidence (i.e. by quoting) from the talk.

1 Native speakers, because they are fluent in English, find few problems in writing in their special subjects.   (   )

_____

_____

_____

2   This talk deals with some of the causes of misunderstandings and breakdowns in written communication.   (   )

_____

_____

_____

3   Short simple sentences are preferable to long complex ones.   (   )

_____

_____

_____

4   Choosing a wrong verb tense will normally cause a breakdown in meaning. (   )

_____

_____

_____

5   A student is advised not to hand in his first attempt at a piece of written work.
                                                                            (   )

_____

_____

_____

Unit 7   Stage 2
Exercise 4   Relative Clauses: Specification in Academic English

A teacher or student when referring to objects and ideas is often required to be detailed and precise. Relative clauses help to achieve this precision in relation to a preceding noun phrase. The table below, when completed, will illustrate how such clauses are formed.

(a) In the column 'Example of a relative clause':
     (i) complete any missing parts by referring to the Stage 2 Text
     (ii) underline the relative clause.
     The first example has been completed for you.

Relative pronoun	Example of a relative clause
1 *who* refers to persons	The student who translates word for word from his first language will not write good English.
2 *which* refers to things	.... he may choose to write sentences _____ _____ complex (see Text)

65

	Relative pronoun	Example of a relative clause
3	*that* also refers to things (and sometimes persons)	It may, therefore, be helpful to analyse the types of error _____ _____ _____ (see Text)
4 5	*whom* (for persons); *which* (for things): both used after prepositions	The lecturer with whom I corresponded will advise me on my research title. The analysis by which the theory was proved is difficult to follow.

(b) From the following table choose an appropriate relative clause to give more detailed information about the relevant noun phrases which appear in the 'Sentence' column. Insert the relative clauses at the points indicated by /.
   Write out the new sentences in full on separate paper.

Sentence	Relative clause
1 The experiment / is almost complete.	**a** who had been unable to buy one in time
2 The student should make an effort in statistics /.	**b** on which he could always rely
3 The lecturer lent his own book to the student /.	**c** which he has not studied before
4 The student / had just passed his examinations.	**d** which was started last year
5 The head of department bought a good computer /.	**e** for whom Dr. Jones was responsible

(c) The extracts below have been taken from students' lecture notes. Write out each extract in full sentence form on separate paper. Each completed sentence should contain a relative clause. The first extract has been done for you.

   1   economists—supported this view—proved wrong.

   > The economists who supported this view were proved wrong.

   2   theory—claims all men equal—v. misleading.
   3   analysis—he tried to prove his theory—v. ingenious.
   4   experiment—his theory was based—complete success.
   5   report—written later—not convincing.
   6   survey—facts were drawn—not cover whole population.

Unit 7 Stage 2
Exercise 5 Correcting Mistakes

The Stage 2 talk referred to some mistakes that students commonly make. If students *check* their written work *carefully* they can correct them themselves.

(a) Each word in brackets below is spelled wrongly. Write the word correctly in the space provided. An example has been done for you.

e.g. (devided) _____divided_____

1 (acommodation) _____
2 (begining) _____
3 (critisism) _____
4 (divelopement) _____
5 (dissapeared) _____
6 (forienger) _____
7 (goverment) _____
8 (necesary) _____
9 (occured) _____
10 (writting) _____
11 (intresting) _____
12 (studing) _____

(b) Each of the sentences below contains *at least one mistake* (*not* a spelling mistake). (i) Underline the part of the sentence that is wrong and then (ii) write the whole sentence correctly beneath it. The first one has been done for you.

1 He was <u>much</u> interested in the explanation.
   He was very interested in the explanation..

2 He attend to seminars every Monday and Thursday afternoon.
_____

3 Some students was very late.
_____

4 The tutor gave the student some useful advices.
_____

5 What this means? He do not know.
_____

6 Psychology is one of social sciences.
_____

7 He applied study chemistry, no physics.
_____

8 He had been doing a research during two years.
_____

9 The student have learned a lot from her lectures.
_____

10 The informations he received was wrong.
_____

11 Seems that the experiment a success.
_____

67

12   These student should succeeds, if he learn to write accurately the English.

Unit 7   Stage 3   Guided Note-taking

Complete the following as you listen to the Stage 3 talk.

Title: . . . .
Writing = ...

Three . . . . :
   1   → misunderstanding or . . . .
       . . . .

     Causes:
       (i) . . . .
           ∴ try to employ . . . .
           . . . .

           Eventually . . . .
           Vocab.: . . . .
                 — misuse Eng. words . . . .
           . . . .
      (ii) Confuse gram. patterns . . . .
          . . . .
          e.g. . . . .
      (iii) Sentences = ...
          ∵. . . . .
          Rule = ...
          . . . .
      (iv) Sentences = ...
          e.g. . . . .

   2   → irritates & . . . .
      e.gs. 1 . . . .
           2 concord
           3 . . . .
           4 . . . .
      ∴ prepare . . . .

   3   _____
      Synonyms = ...
               e.g. . . . .
          . . . .
      Equally . . . .

New abbreviations used above:
gram. = grammatical

Unit 7   Stage 3   Alternative Guided Note-taking

Listen to the Stage 3 talk and take notes using the lecturer's signals (listed below) to help you. These can be written in the book or on a separate piece of paper.

Lecturer's signals	Notes
It may prove helpful, therefore, if I outline	. . . .
I'll also try to suggest . . . and	. . . .
Firstly, and most seriously	(1) . . . .
. . . are numerous and I'll therefore be able to do no more than try to cover the most important ones here.	
Perhaps the most frequent cause	(i) . . . .
. . . therefore	. . . .
Eventually	. . . .
But it's not only	(a) . . . .
. . . too	(b) . . . .
Another factor which is at work here is as follows	. . . .
Another very important cause . . .	(ii) . . . .
For example	. . . .
A third cause	(iii) . . . .
. . . therefore	. . . .
In particular	. . . .
. . . a fourth cause	(iv) . . . .
For example	. . . .
The second main type of error . .	(2) . . . .
. . . falls into this category.	(i) . . . .
Then	(ii) . . . .
	(iii) . . . .
	(iv) . . . .
. . . therefore	. . . .
Finally, we come to the third type of error	(3) . . . .
. . . for instance	. . . .
Equally	. . . .

Unit 7   Stage 3   Follow-up Activity 1*

Oral Reconstruction and Checking/Completion of Notes
See Unit 2: Stage 3: Follow-up Activity 1 for procedure.

Follow-up Activity 2*

Discussion
1   (i)   Which of the problems described by the lecturer do you encounter when writing in English?
    (ii)   Do you experience any other difficulties? If so, what are they?
    (iii)   List the *five* most serious problems identified in (i) and (ii) above in order of severity, beginning with what you consider to be your greatest source of difficulty when writing in English.
2   Working in groups of 3 or 4:
    (i)   compare your lists of problems of writing in English. Tick (√) any problems which are shared by *two or more* group members.
    (ii)   Draw up a group list of the problems identified in 2(i) above. Indicate (in brackets) how many people encounter each of the problems listed.
    (iii)   One member from each group should now write the group list on the blackboard in the following manner:

Group _____		Group _____
Problem	Frequency of Occurrence	etc.
1.		
2.		
3.		
4.		
5.		

3   With the help of your teacher draw up a class list of the *five* problems most frequently encountered when writing in English.

Follow-up Activity 3*

Writing
Write two paragraphs on *The Problems of Writing in English*.
The first should summarize the problems of writing in a foreign language described in the talk.
The second should report briefly on the survey conducted above.
Begin your paragraphs as follows:

Paragraph 1:
It is generally anticipated that the learner of English will encounter the following problems in his/her writing. Firstly,..
Paragraph 2:
A survey was conducted of the writing problems faced by a group of students on the _____ course at _____.
The five most frequently encountered problems were as follows.
_____ students have difficulty with _____ when writing in English . . .

70

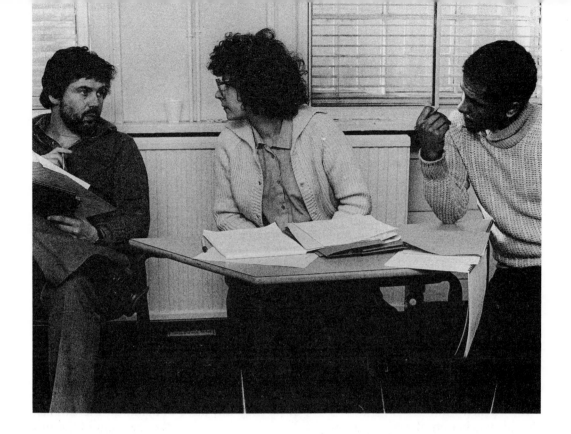

UNIT 8
THE IMPORTANCE OF QUESTIONS

Unit 8   Stage 1   Dictation
(The Text is in the *Key to the Exercises*, at the back of the book.)

Either the tape of Stage 1 can be played, and a pause button used to give time to write on paper, or the teacher can read the Text as a dictation.

Unit 8   Stage 2
Exercise 1   Listening Comprehension

Read the following sentences and as you listen to the Stage 2 talk decide whether they are true or false *according to the passage*. Write T (true) or F (false) in the brackets ( ) after each sentence.

1 Discussion work has limited value for the student who is not good at asking questions.   ( )
2 The teacher may think a student's question is a statement if the correct grammatical form is not used.   ( )
3 The teacher must make certain that he is clear about the exact reference of a student's question.   ( )
4 The student's question on 'cost inflation' is considered a bad one.   ( )
5 Absence of the interrogative form may cause a student to sound impolite.   ( )

71

Unit 8   Stage 2
Exercise 2   Listening and Blank-filling

Complete the following by writing *one or more words* in each space as you listen to the talk.

THE IMPORTANCE OF QUESTIONS

1 In order to obtain full value from a group discussion, a student must be good
2 _____ questions. If he isn't, then any attempt he makes to resolve his
3 difficulties may _____ further confusion.
4   A very frequent source of misunderstanding in a discussion is, in fact, the teacher's
5 uncertainty _____ his student has, indeed, asked a question _____
6 _____ . What often happens is _____ . The student, puzzled about
7 a particular point, decides to ask a question. Unfortunately he concentrates all his
8 attention on the subject matter and _____ the language. Consequently,
9 he fails to employ the correct grammatical form. The result is _____ .
10 The teacher interprets the intended question as a comment. He either agrees or
11 disagrees with it, or he continues _____ he was saying before.
12   However, _____ the student does employ an appropriate question
13 form, difficulties may still _____ . The teacher may not know, for
14 example, _____ of the student's difficulty. The student may not have
15 clearly heard what _____ ; or he may not have understood the English
16 that his teacher employed; or he may not _____ the meaning of a point
17 in relation to his special subject. Each of _____ difficulties _____
18 _____ a different kind of question.
19   Next, a student _____ that his teacher is clear about exactly which
20 point he is referring to. In order to be absolutely _____ , it's a good
21 idea for students to _____ their questions with an introductory state-
22 ment, for example, 'I don't understand the point you made at the beginning of the
23 discussion about cost inflation. Could you explain it again please?' The teacher is
24 then _____ to give a satisfactory answer without any waste of time.
25 Furthermore, when a student asks questions on a text he must be very careful to
26 locate the _____ .
27   Finally, it should be mentioned that it's often necessary to employ a question
28 form because *not* to do so would be rude.

Unit 8   Stage 2
Exercise 3   Reading Comprehension

Read the following sentences and as you read the text above (see Exercise 2) decide if they are true or false *according to the passage*. You must (i) write T or F in the brackets and (ii) justify your answer, in the space provided, by giving evidence (i.e. by quoting) from the talk.

1   It is advisable for a student to focus all his attention on the subject matter when
he is involved in a discussion.   (   )

_____

_____

_____

2   A breakdown in communication is likely to occur when a student fails to use
    the correct grammatical form of a question.   (   )

    _____

    _____

    _____

3   A student who has learned to use question forms correctly has no further problems
    with asking questions.   (   )

    _____

    _____

    _____

4   The use of an appropriate background statement before a question helps to make
    an enquiry more specific.   (   )

    _____

    _____

    _____

5   A teacher is not normally in a position to give suitable answers to questions
    unless they are precise.   (   )

    _____

    _____

    _____

Unit 8   Stage 2
Exercise 4   Purpose

(a) The intended result or purpose of an action is often described by the construction:
    in order to + verb stem, e.g.

(i) | *In order to obtain* full value from a group discussion, a student must be good at asking questions. | (line 1–2)

    Now find one more example from the talk and write it below:

    _____

    _____

    _____

(ii) The following construction is also possible in which the purpose follows
     the statement:

     A student must be good at asking questions *in order to obtain* full value from a group discussion.

(b) Instead of using *in order to + verb stem* it is equally possible to use *to + verb stem* or, especially in informal English, *so as to + verb stem*.

Using the table below match a Statement with the appropriate Purpose; insert *in order to, to* or *so as to*. Write out the sentences on separate paper.

Statement	Purpose
1 The student must ask precise questions	**a** avoid making unnecessary mistakes.
2 Many academic courses try to provide a number of tutorials	**b** give the students enough time to write it down.
3 A student should aim to write in simple English	**c** save time when writing his notes.
4 A student must know how to abbreviate	**d** get clear answers.
5 A good lecturer will often repeat an important point	**e** give students the opportunity to ask questions and clear up their difficulties.

(c) Now write sentences of your own based on the following information. Add a suitable *purpose*, e.g.

Use the dictionary →
He should use the dictionary in order to look up new words.

1 take notes →_____

_____

2 read as widely as possible →_____

_____

3 check written work carefully →_____

_____

4 use a language laboratory →_____

_____

5 learn to use a library catalogue →_____

_____

Unit 8   Stage 2
Exercise 5   Asking for Repetition or an Explanation

The Stage 2 talk emphasized the importance of asking precise questions. The table below summarizes ways in which questions may be asked in order to get a repetition or an explanation of some item not previously understood.

Look carefully at the table. Remember that each question should begin with a *polite request: 'Excuse me, please could you....'*

Required action	*Required item*	*Time reference*	*Topic reference*	*Mode of repetition*
repeat	the last sentence			more clearly?
explain	the reference you made what you said	just now a minute ago at the beginning	about: cost inflation (?) state planning (?) the percentage involved (?)	more loudly? more slowly?
explain	what you meant the reference		the rate of illiteracy (?)	
write	the author's name you mentioned the book title you gave			on the blackboard?

e.g. Excuse me, please could you repeat what you said just now about the rate of illiteracy more slowly?

Now you compose another *5 questions* from the table and write them on separate paper.

Unit 8   Stage 3   Guided Note-taking

Complete the following as you listen to the Stage 3 talk.

Title: ....

Group discussions = ...
   BUT must be ....

1   In early stages
     Explans.: (i) ....
             (ii) ....
            (iii) v. frequent cause = ...
                 —fails to ....
                 e.g. ....

                   ....

2   Even when st. employs approp. Q. form
    e.g. source ....
        Differ. types: (a) ....
                  (b) ....
                  (c) ....
        Each type reqs. ....

3   Q. must be
    To be precise = ...
                    ....
          → Teacher in position ....
                    ....
    Q. on text — ....

4   Correct Q. form imp. — nec. not to be ....
      S'times ....
                 ....
      Imp. ∴ ....

New abbreviations used above:

Explans.	= explanations	reqs.	= requires
freq.	= frequent	nec.	= necessary
approp.	= appropriate		

Unit 8   Stage 3   Alternative Guided Note-taking

Listen to the Stage 3 talk and take notes using the lecturer's signals (listed below) to help you. These can be written in the book or on a separate piece of paper.

Lecturer's signals	Notes
(Title)	. . . .
. . . there are frequent	(1) . . . .
There are, of course, many	. . . .
	(i) . . . .
. . . on the other hand	(ii) . . . .
But a very frequent cause	(iii) . . . .
For example	. . . .
However	. . . .
. . . for example	. . . .
The basic difficulty may, in fact, be one of several different types . . .	(i) . . . .
. . . or	(ii) . . . .
. . . or alternatively	(iii) . . . .
	(2) . . . .
	(i) . . . .
Next	(ii) . . . .
	(a) . . . .
Perhaps, before concluding, one further example may be helpful . .	(b) . . . .
Finally, one point that should be mentioned before we leave this subject	(iii) . . . .

Note: For (2) above you will have to provide your own heading since the lecturer does not signal one.

Unit 8   Stage 3   Follow-up Activity 1*

Comprehension Check

This time, you are going to ask the questions.

1   Read through your notes and identify any omissions/points of uncertainty.

2   Try to construct a question for each omission/point of uncertainty.
     e.g. 'What was the second type of difficulty mentioned by the lecturer?'

3   See if the rest of the class (or your teacher) can answer your questions.

Follow-up Activity 2*

Asking questions about a text

Your teacher will provide you with a text for this exercise (see *Key and Notes to the Follow-up Activities*, p.143).

1   Read through the text and make a note of any difficulties the text presents.

2   Using the following structure to help you, ask the rest of the class if they can help you with your difficulties.

Could you please explain	the meaning of what is meant by	the	word _____ phrase _____ sentence beginning _____
in	line _____? the (third) line of the (second) paragraph?		
(two) lines from the bottom at the end beginning		of the (fourth) paragraph?	

UNIT 9
GROUP DISCUSSIONS

Unit 9   Stage 1   Dictation
(The Text is in the *Key to the Exercises*, at the back of the book.)

Either the tape of Stage 1 can be played, and a pause button used to give time to write on paper, or the teacher can read the Text as a dictation.

Unit 9   Stage 2
Exercise 1   Listening Comprehension

Read the following sentences and as you listen to the Stage 2 talk decide whether they are true or false *according to the passage*. Write T (true) or F (false) in the brackets ( ) after each sentence.

1 Group discussions are frequently called seminars and tutorials.   ( )
2 A tutorial was usually for twenty-five students.   ( )
3 There are clear differences in purpose between seminars and tutorials.   ( )
4 Group discussions only deal with problems that the student may have found in following his lectures.   ( )
5 Non-native speakers do not find it easy to benefit from group discussions. ( )

Unit 9   Stage 2
Exercise 2   Listening and Blank-filling

Complete the following by writing *one or more words* in each space as you listen to the talk.

GROUP DISCUSSIONS

1   Today ⎯⎯⎯⎯⎯ to talk about group discussions. In an academic context
2   these are often known as 'seminars' and 'tutorials'. Firstly, I want to consider the
3   meaning of ⎯⎯⎯⎯⎯, then look at the aims of group discussions and
4   finally ⎯⎯⎯⎯⎯ some of the problems learners of English may have in
5   work of this kind.
6   Firstly, then, the meaning of the terms 'seminar' and 'tutorial'. Originally
7   ⎯⎯⎯⎯⎯ clear differences in size and in purpose between a 'seminar' and
8   'tutorial'. A tutorial was usually for ⎯⎯⎯⎯⎯ students whereas a seminar
9   was attended by about ten to fifteen. In a tutorial a lecturer ⎯⎯⎯⎯⎯
10   answered questions related to his recent lecture ⎯⎯⎯⎯⎯ in a seminar one
11   student would usually give a short talk which ⎯⎯⎯⎯⎯ an introduction to
12   a more general discussion. However, nowadays these terms are often employed
13   interchangeably. Therefore the term 'group discussion' will be used ⎯⎯⎯⎯⎯.
14   Turning now to the general aims of group discussions, I want to mention the
15   two most important ⎯⎯⎯⎯⎯. The main aim is that (and I quote from a
16   survey) 'students should ⎯⎯⎯⎯⎯ to discuss and to clarify difficulties
17   ⎯⎯⎯⎯⎯ lectures or other teaching sessions'. During a lecture students
18   ⎯⎯⎯⎯⎯ usually expected to interrupt to ask questions. The second
19   objective is, and I ⎯⎯⎯⎯⎯, 'to obtain more intimate and personal contact
20   with students than is possible in lectures'. In smaller groups this is, of course,
21   ⎯⎯⎯⎯⎯.
22   Group discussions, if ⎯⎯⎯⎯⎯ properly exploited by students, can be
23   highly stimulating and extremely beneficial. Yet it's difficult, especially for non-native
24   speakers, to take full advantage ⎯⎯⎯⎯⎯. There are many reasons
25   ⎯⎯⎯⎯⎯. I'll just mention three which I think are particularly important.
26   Firstly, ⎯⎯⎯⎯⎯ which takes place may be very fast. Secondly, a student
27   may not know how to break into a discussion politely. The third ⎯⎯⎯⎯⎯
28   difficulty is how to formulate questions quickly and accurately.

Unit 9   Stage 2
Exercise 3   Reading Comprehension

Read the following sentences and as you read the text above (see Exercise 2) decide if they are true or false *according to the passage*. You must (i) write T or F in the brackets and (ii) justify your answer, in the space provided, by giving evidence (i.e. by quoting) from the talk.

1   The speaker has two main objectives in his talk.   ( )

    _____

    _____

    _____

2 The speaker intends to analyse in great detail the problems that non-native speakers of English may encounter in group discussions.   ( )

_____

_____

_____

3 Historically, the seminar consisted of a very small number of students discussing a recent lecture with their tutor.   ( )

_____

_____

_____

4 The most important aim of group discussions is to allow the tutor and his students to get to know each other better.   ( )

_____

_____

_____

5 There are just three reasons why it is difficult for students to take advantage of group discussions.   ( )

_____

_____

_____

Unit 9   Stage 2
Exercise 4   Relationship between Ideas: Connectives

Frequently a lecturer tries to help the listener follow easily what he is saying by showing the relationship between various statements he makes. The table below illustrates some of the ways in which this is achieved and the *connectives* commonly used.

+relationship (='and')			−relationship (='but')
enumeration	addition	result	concession
Firstly Secondly Then Later Finally	Moreover Furthermore In addition Again	Therefore Thus	However Yet Nevertheless In spite of (this/that)

(a) Now study the Stage 2 Text and, in the table below, give examples of the relationships listed by writing the *connectives* (together with their line numbers). If no examples occur write NIL. Some examples have been done for you.

	Relationship	Connective(s) used (and line numbers)
(i)	enumeration	Firstly (2), then (3), finally (4)
(ii)	enumeration	
(iii)	addition	
(iv)	result	
(v)	concession	

(b) Complete the spaces in the paragraph below with appropriate *connectives* from the first table above (on page 67).

Students find group discussions difficult. They frequently withdraw, (i) _____ , and make little attempt to join in. (ii) _____ , there is no doubt that discussion can be very valuable if properly exploited. (iii) _____ , it will be worthwhile suggesting how the student can tackle this problem. It will, (iv) _____ , certainly be worthwhile convincing him that improvement in this area is vital to his progress.

(c) Complete the following with sentences of your own:

1 The lecture was very difficult. However, _____

_____

2 The time available for asking questions was very short. Nevertheless, _____

_____

3 The text-book covered all the main points. Furthermore, _____

_____

4 The report was checked and re-checked. Thus, _____

_____

Unit 9   Stage 2
Exercise 5   Contrast

(a) In the talk *whereas* is used to contrast the ideas contained in two clauses, e.g.,

A tutorial was usually for two to five students *whereas* a seminar was attended by about ten to fifteen.	(line 8–9)

In place of *whereas* it is equally possible to use *while* (or, less commonly, *whilst*).

The clause introduced by *whereas* may also begin the sentence (sometimes causing minor changes), e.g.,

> Whereas a seminar was attended by about ten to fifteen students, a tutorial was usually for two to five.

Now find one more example from the talk and write it below:

_____

_____

_____

(b) Write sentences of your own to contrast the following pairs of words. Use _whereas_ or _while_, either at the beginning of the sentence or in the middle of the two clauses.

e.g. _undergraduate/postgraduate_:
An undergraduate studies for a first degree whereas a postgraduate studies
for a higher qualification.

1   _encyclopedia/text-book_: _____

_____

_____

2   _Contents/Index_: _____

_____

_____

3   _footnote/title_: _____

_____

_____

4   _lecture/seminar_: _____

_____

_____

5   _essay/thesis_: _____

_____

_____

Unit 9   Stage 3   Guided Note-taking

Complete the following as you listen to the Stage 3 talk.

Title: . . . .

In acad. context = ...

      1 . . . .   2 . . . .

      3 . . . .   4 . . . .

  1   Terms — trad. differs. = (i) . . . .
                         (ii) . . . .

     Tut. = ...   Sem. = ...
     Tut. = ...
            . . . .
     Sem. = ...
            . . . .
     Survey in . . . . by Dr. Ruth Beard . . . .
                                       . . . .
     → some lecturers use . . . .
                              . . . .
     ∴ using . . . .

  2   Two most ‾‾‾‾‾‾‾‾‾‾‾‾‾‾‾‾‾‾‾‾‾‾‾‾‾‾‾‾‾‾‾‾‾‾‾‾‾‾‾
     (i) . . . .
         . . . .
     (ii) . . . .
     Other aims: (a) . . . .
                (b) . . . . etc.

  3   Diffs. — imp.:
     (i) . . . .
     (ii) . . . .
     (iii) . . . .
     (iv) . . . .

  4   Advice:
     (i) . . . .
         . . . .
     (ii) Altho' gram. accuracy IS imp., ...
         . . . .

New abbreviations used above:

acad. = academic   sem.   = seminar
trad. = traditional   Altho' = although
tut.   = tutorial

Unit 9 Stage 3 Alternative Guided Note-taking

Listen to the Stage 3 talk and take notes using the lecturer's signals (listed below) to help you. These can be written in the book or on a separate piece of paper.

Lecturer's signals	Notes
Today I'd like to talk to you about	. . . .
I want first of all to deal with . . .	(1) . . . .
. . . then I want to cover	(2) . . . .
. . . next I'll go on to look at	(3) . . . .
. . . and then finally I'd like to	(4) . . . .
Firstly, then, let's look at	(1) . . . .
. . . firstly	(i) . . . .
. . . secondly, and perhaps more importantly	(ii) . . . .
. . . whereas	. . . .
. . . on the other hand	. . . .
These are, as I've pointed out . . .	. . . .
However	. . . .
From now on I also intend to use	. . . .
Let's now turn to	(2) . . . .
I want to mention	. . . .
. . . afterwards I'll mention	. . . .
In the first place	(i) . . . .
The second most important objective is	(ii) . . . .
Other more specific aims . . . include	(iii) . . . .
Yet	(3) . . . .
There are many . . . . I'll just mention four which I think are particularly important.	. . . .
Firstly	(i) . . . .
Secondly	(ii) (a) . . . .
Furthermore	(b) . . . .
The third major difficulty	(iii) . . . .
Fourthly	(iv) . . . .
So what advice can be given . . .?.	(4) . . . .
. . . the first thing to do	(i) . . . .
Secondly	(ii) . . . .

Unit 9   Stage 3   Follow-up Activity 1*

Requesting Clarification

In Units 1 and 4 you practised clarifying any omissions/points of uncertainty by asking the rest of the class or the teacher.

Very often, however, you will be able to resolve any such difficulties by asking a fellow student rather more informally (i.e. without having to address a large group of people).

e.g. | 'Did you catch | what the lecturer said about _____?'
| | the (fourth problem) the lecturer mentioned?'

| 'What did you get down about _____?'

1   Working with a fellow student see if you can help one another, in this more informal manner, with any clarification necessary.

2   If necessary, ask the rest of the class (or the teacher) for any further clarification (see Unit 1: Stage 3: Follow-up Activity 1).

Follow-up Activity 2*

Oral Reconstruction/Speaking from Notes

In Units 2, 5 and 7 you practised reconstructing the talk from your notes as a means of checking their accuracy and completeness.

The ability to speak fluently and coherently from a set of notes is, however, an important study skill in itself, particularly in seminars. In this and the next Unit you have a further opportunity to practise this skill.

1   Read through your notes, making sure you have satisfactorily resolved any difficulties.

2   Consider how you might do the following:

  (i) introduce the subject of the talk.

  (ii) mark the transition from one part of the talk to the next.

  You can, of course, make use of the lecturer's signals from this particular talk. Alternatively, you may wish to refer to the lists of signals you made in Unit 3.

3   Your teacher will now ask individual members of the class to reconstruct a small part of the talk. Remember to link your part of the talk to the previous one using an appropriate signal.

Follow-up Activity 3*

Discussion

1   Consider the following questions. You may find it useful to make one or two notes.

  (i) What role, if any, do group discussions play within the university/college system in your country?

  (ii) Does there exist a distinction similar to that drawn between the 'tutorial' and the 'seminar' in Britain? If so, what is the basis for such a distinction?

2   Working in groups of 3 or 4 discuss your answers to the above. Can you make any generalisations about the role of group discussions within different university/college systems?

3   One member from each group should now share with the rest of the class any generalisations made.

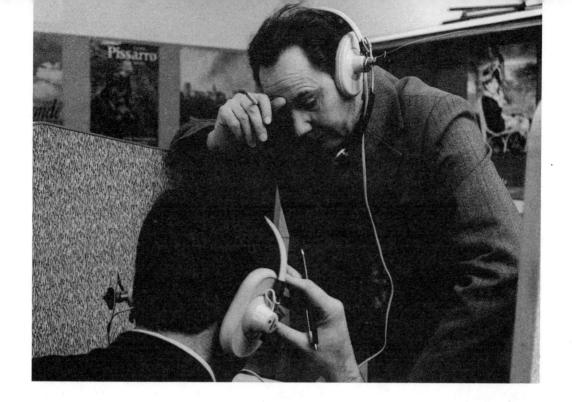

UNIT 10
LEARNING A LANGUAGE

Unit 10   Stage 1   Dictation
(The Text is in the *Key to the Exercises*, at the back of the book.)

Either the tape of Stage 1 can be played, and a pause button used to give time to write on paper, or the teacher can read the Text as a dictation.

Unit 10   Stage 2
Exercise 1   Listening Comprehension

Read the following sentences and as you listen to the Stage 2 talk decide whether they are true or false *according to the passage*. Write T (true) or F (false) in the brackets ( ) after each sentence.

1   The speaker says that this last talk is a serious lecture.   ( )
2   Progress is probably slow in foreign language learning.   ( )
3   The student makes many linguistic errors when he is under pressure.   ( )
4   The student controls the language, rather than the language controlling the student.   ( )
5   The ways in which a student can help himself in language learning can be grouped in three categories.   ( )

Unit 10   Stage 2
Exercise 2   Listening and Blank-filling

Complete the following by writing *one or more words* in each space as you listen to the talk.

LEARNING A LANGUAGE

1 For this last talk in this _____ lectures I'm going to discuss learning a
2 language. I shall deal with the basic problems first and then _____ to
3 suggest various possible solutions. The students I have in mind here are those who
4 _____ learning English in order to begin a course of studies _____
5 _____ in that medium.
6   Probably the most fundamental problem that the student _____ is
7 the feeling that the problem is _____ great for him. Difficulties occur
8 on all sides and progress can be very slight. The _____ reading in his
9 own subject slows down and his comprehension becomes less secure. In addition, he
10 expresses himself slowly and he often _____ convey his ideas exactly.
11 He's disappointed, _____, to find that under pressure he makes a lot
12 of unnecessary mistakes _____ where he knows the correct language
13 forms. Again, his social relations are difficult as he cannot always find the right
14 phrase quickly _____ to keep a conversation going. Instead of the
15 student being in control of the language, the language seems now to be in control of
16 the student.
17   _____ can be very depressing and the student can start to feel very
18 _____. Working in a foreign language is also very tiring, and the
19 concentration and self-discipline required to correct _____ mistakes is
20 very great indeed.
21   But what _____ done about the problems? Well, _____
22 many ways in which the student can help himself. It might be helpful if we
23 _____ under three broad headings. Firstly, the student _____
24 himself a number of realistic _____. Secondly, he must work out an
25 appropriate method of study. Thirdly, he must try to adopt a set of attitudes which
26 _____ progress.

Unit 10   Stage 2
Exercise 3   Reading Comprehension

Read the following sentences and as you read the text above (see Exercise 2)
decide if they are true or false *according to the passage*. You must (i) write T or F
in the brackets and (ii) justify your answer, in the space provided, by giving evidence
(i.e. by quoting) from the talk.

1   The students that the speaker is concerned with are those who have been learning
    a subject through the medium of English.   (   )

_____

_____

_____

2   The basic problem for the student is that he feels that the problem of learning English, while not impossibly difficult, is certainly very great.   ( )

_____

_____

_____

3   Contact with people is not affected by a student's slow or hesitant speech.   ( )

_____

_____

_____

4   The concentration and self-discipline necessary to correct one's own mistakes is, in fact, too great for the student.   ( )

_____

_____

_____

5   The student can help to tackle his problems and can make effective progress by setting himself a number of very high aims.   ( )

_____

_____

_____

Unit 10   Stage 2
Exercise 4   Comparison: *'Too'* and *'Enough'*

Comparisons are often made to a norm or a desired standard.

1   If the item being compared reaches the norm, the construction with *enough* may be used (indicating 'sufficiency').
2   If it fails to reach the norm, *not enough* may be used (indicating 'insufficiency').
3   If it exceeds the norm, and becomes undesirable, *too* may be used (indicating 'excess').

e.g. There were seats for 50 students in the lecture room. (statement = norm)

1   Fifty students came to the lecture.
    There were *enough* seats for all of them. (=sufficiency)
2   A hundred students came to the lecture.
    There were *not enough* seats for all of them. (=insufficiency)
3   A hundred students came to the lecture.
    There were *too* many students in the room: (=excess)
    they could not all sit down.

(a) In the Stage 2 Text there are two examples of the above forms of comparison. Write below the *phrases* containing the words and label them correctly (i.e. sufficiency, insufficiency or excess).

1 _____

2 _____

(b) Construct meaningful sentences from the parts given in the table below. The first sentence has been done for you. Write the remainder on separate paper.

1	The lecturer spoke slowly enough	**a**	to hold the student's interest.
2	The book did not contain enough information	**b**	for the audience to understand.
3	The application was far too late	**c**	for it to be finished on time.
4	The experiment encountered too many difficulties	**d**	to pay for a new building.
5	The college had enough money	**e**	for him to want to buy it.
6	The work was not varied enough	**f**	for the student to be accepted.

e.g. 1   The lecturer spoke slowly enough for the audience to understand.

(c) Use the appropriate construction—'too', '(not) enough'—with the word in brackets in order to complete the following sentences. The first one has been done for you.

(*fast*)   1   If a student's reading speed is *not fast enough* he will have difficulty in reading all the recommended books.

(*precise*)   2   If a student asks a question which is _____, he will waste a lot of time.

(*carefully*)   3   If a student checks his essays _____, he will be able to correct most of his mistakes himself.

(*pressure*)   4   If a student is put under _____, he will tend to make a lot of errors.

(*ambitious*)   5   If the targets a student sets himself are _____, he will end up confused and disappointed.

(*positive*)   6   If the attitudes a student adopts are _____, he will make considerable progress.

NOTE: There is a difference in meaning between *too* and *very*:
        This problem is *very* difficult. (But I *can* just do it.)
        This problem is *too* difficult. (So I *cannot* do it.)

Unit 10   Stage 2
Exercise 5   Revision: Missing Words

In each line one word has been deliberately omitted. You must
 (i) decide which word is missing
 (ii) indicate by a stroke (/) where it should go
(iii) write the word to the left of the vertical line.
The first word has been done for you.

_____a_____	1	When / student studies in the medium of a foreign
_____	2	language, it sometimes to him that the problems
_____	3	are great to be solved. Instead of the student
_____	4	being in control of the language, the seems now
_____	5	to be in control of the student. Seminars and
_____	6	tutorials may help the speaker to solve his
_____	7	problems, the non-native speaker is likely find
_____	8	that he is skilful enough in asking questions to
_____	9	be able to gain real benefit these sessions. He
_____	10	should pay special attention to this area language
_____	11	learning so to ensure that he can join in
_____	12	discussions and clear up any he may have.

Unit 10　Stage 3　Guided Note-taking

Complete the following as you listen to the Stage 3 talk.

Title: . . . .

　　<u>1　Basic probs.</u>

　　2　. . . . .

1　Most fund. prob. = ...

　　Now Eng. = med. of instr. →

　　　　— unknown . . . .

　　　　— diffs. with . . . .

　　　　— reading . . . .

　　　　　　　　　. . . . . etc. etc.

　　　　— social relations = ...

　　Lang. seems . . . . etc.

2　<u>St. can help self:</u>

　　　　(1) . . . .

　　　　(2) . . . .

　　　　(3) . . . .

　　(1)　Targets — REALISTIC! = most imp. → immed. short-term:

　　　　Personal　　= . . . .

　　　　. . . . . = ...

　　　　. . . . . = ...

　　　　　　　　　　　. . . . .

　　　　e.g. Every day　　. . . . .

　　　　　　　　　　　. . . . .

　　(2)　Method — systematic, thoro', ...

　　　　e.g. . . . .

　　　　　Write:　(i) . . . .

　　　　　　　　(ii) . . . .

　　　　　　　　(iii) . . . . (optional)

　　　　　Learned 3 ways:

　　　　　　　　(i) . . . .

　　　　　　　　(ii) mnemonic . . . .

　　　　　　　　(iii) . . . .

　　　　　　　　. . . . . = pract. e.g.

　　　　　St. should . . . .

　　　　　— daily . . . .

　　(3)　Progress in lang. = most likely if . . . .

　　　　. . . . .

New abbreviations used above:

fund. = fundamental	immed. = immediate
med. = medium	thoro' = thorough
instr. = instruction	pract. = practical

Unit 10   Stage 3   Alternative Guided Note-taking

Listen to the Stage 3 talk and take notes using the lecturer's signals (listed below) to help you. These can be written in the book or on a separate piece of paper.

Lecturer's signals	Notes
...I'm going to discuss	....
I shall deal with...first	(1) ....
and then I'll go on to suggest ...	(2) ....
Probably the most fundamental problem......................	(1) ....
	....
	....
	....
But what can be done about these problems?...Well, there are many ways	(2) ....
It might be helpful if we deal with them under three broad headings.	
Firstly	(i) ....
Secondly	(ii) ....
Thirdly	(iii) ....
First then	(i) ....
This is *most* important.	
What do we mean by this? By...we mean	....
By...we mean	....
By...we mean	....
A practical example may be helpful here	....
Next, though, we must consider	(ii) ....
It may be helpful if we again illustrate this	....
Three items of information...	
firstly	(a) ....
secondly	(b) ....
thirdly	(c) ....
This last item is optional...	

93

In the final analysis ....|...

                         (a) ....

                         (b) ....

                         (c) ....

Let's take ... as a practical example | ....

                         ....

... also ....   (d) ....

Finally ....   (iii) ....

... therefore ....|...

Unit 10   Stage 3   Follow-up Activity 1*

Requesting Clarification
See Unit 9: Stage 3: Follow-up Activity 1 for procedure.

Follow-up Activity 2*

Oral Reconstruction/Speaking from Notes
See Unit 9: Stage 3: Follow-up Activity 2 for procedure.

Follow-up Activity 3*

Writing
Use your notes to write a 250–300 word summary of the talk.

KEY TO THE EXERCISES

CONTENTS

The Key to the 10 Units is set out in the following sequence for each Unit:

STAGE 1   Text

              Notes. A summary is laid out on page 96.

STAGE 2   Key to the Exercises

STAGE 3   Suggested Notes

              Text

Note: (1) The Text of Stage 2 is to be found in each Unit in *Exercise 2* (when it is completed), located in the front section of the book.

        (2) The phonetic symbols used in the Notes for Stage 1 are the same as those used in *The Advanced Learner's Dictionary of Current English* by A. S. Hornby (O.U.P.). The phonetic symbols used in the *Collins English Learner's Dictionary* by D. J. Carver, M. J. Wallace and J. Cameron (Collins) are slightly different.

STAGE 1 NOTES: SUMMARY OF CONTENTS

UNIT	PRONUNCIATION	STRUCTURE	VOCABULARY
1	weak forms; plurals /s/s/ɪz	prep. + verb stem + ing	punctuation
2	weak forms; contractions; plurals /s/z/	advs. of frequency; find + it + adj. + to do something	to listen to follow the argument such as
3	syllable stress; unstressed syllables	have to do something	as . . . . to write . . . . down
4	final consonant sounds; main stress	think that + clause; every word has	to hold . . . . views nearly to be in a position to
5	/i/ɪ/ main stress; extra strong stress	poss. adj. + verb stem + ing; prep. + verb stem + ing; no/not	have . . . . in mind
6	/v/w/ dropping unstressed syllables	modal: may; article: a/the; purpose	shelf/shelves various borrow from aspects
7	/ð/θ/	preps. after verbs; relative clauses; gerund	to master broad error misunderstanding
8	rising intonation; dropping unstressed syllables; '-ed': /d/ɪd/t/	purpose clauses; be + adj. + at + verb stem + ing + something	likely ensure source be clear about involved
9	consonant sounds	passives; differences in/ between . . . . ; introductory 'there'	context nowadays terms enable
10	extra strong word stress	revision	series have in mind (style)

Unit 1   Stage 1   Text

SOME OF THE PROBLEMS FACING LEARNERS OF ENGLISH

1 The problems which face learners of English can be divided into three categories:
2 psychological, cultural and linguistic. The largest category seems to be linguistic.
3   As regards linguistic factors, students often have great difficulty in understanding
4 spoken English. Possible reasons are:
5   Firstly, it seems that English people speak very quickly.
6   Secondly, they speak with a variety of accents.
7   Thirdly, different styles of speech are used.

Unit 1   Stage 1   Notes

(Figures in brackets refer to line numbers above.)

1 *PRONUNCIATION*
   (a) *weak forms*
     (1) of /əv/ ; can be /kən bɪ/
     (2) and /ən(d)/ ; the /ðə/
     (2) to be /tə bɪ/
     (3) as /əz/ ; have /həv/
     (5) that /ðət/
     (6) a /ə/ ; of /əv/
     (7) of /əv/ ; are /ə/

   (b) *plurals* /s/ /z/
     students ⎫
     accents ⎬ /s/
     problems ⎫
     learners
     categories
     seems ⎬ /z/
     regards
     factors
     reasons
     styles ⎭

Note: although not in this Unit there is another, less common, plural form /ɪz/, e.g. course—courses
     /s/   /sɪz/

2 *STRUCTURE*
   preposition + verb stem + ing....
   (3) in understanding

3 *PUNCTUATION*
   The names of punctuation marks: colon (:)   comma (,)   full-stop (.)
   semi-colon (;)   dash (—)   question mark (?)   exclamation mark (!)
   inverted commas (' ')

Unit 1   Stage 2   Key to the Exercises

(Figures in brackets refer to line numbers in the Text in Exercise 2, located in the front section of the book.)

Exercise 1
1 F (4–5)
2 T (7–8; 13)

3 F (26–27)
4 T (28–29)
5 F (31–32)

Exercise 2

(1) I'd (3) tongue (4) can be (6) I'll (8) of the (9) studies (11) are of
(11) e.g. (13) Let's (14) will have had (18) for this (20) of accents
(22) practice (24) language (25) listen (28) fluently (29) it's
(30) that he can (31) he must (33) to as much
Note: Vocabulary
(15) pract*ise* (verb) (22) pract*ice* (noun): same pronunciation, different spelling

Exercise 3

1 T I'll comment only briefly on these two categories. (6)
2 F .... *some* of them are of a very practical nature. (10–11)
3 F I'll just mention three of the *possible* reasons for this. (17–18)
4 F *English people* .... *they* speak with a variety of accents. (19–20)
5 F .... using a language laboratory .... will help (a student) to *think* in English .... (31–34)

Exercise 4

(a) 1 .... they lack everyday practice *in* listen*ing* to English people speaking English. (21–22)
    2 .... the student probably has difficulty *in* speak*ing* English fluently. (28)
(b) following (*or* understanding); understanding (*or* following); listening; speaking; expressing; telling; using; borrowing; asking; reading.

Exercise 5

(a) 1 .... he *should* take every opportunity to meet and speak with native English-speaking people. (26–27)
    2 .... he *must* try to think in English. (31)
(b) (i) 1 He should speak more loudly (when he talks to his tutors).
        2 He should write more carefully (when he does his essays).
        3 He should arrive earlier (for classes and seminars).
   (ii) 4 He should always check his written work (for mistakes in spelling).
        5 He should attend all the lectures (that have been recommended).
        6 He should write up his lecture notes (soon after the lecture has finished).

Unit 1   Stage 3   Guided Note-taking

Suggested notes, completed in italic type.

<u>Title</u>: *Some of probs. facing learners of Eng.*

<u>Purpose</u>: 1 aware *sts. probs.*
          2 suggest *how overcome*

<u>3 categories</u>: 1 *Psychological*
              2 Cultural
              3 *Linguistic*
        1 Some = fear *of unknown* e.g. *academic studies too difficult?* Also *separation from family*, poss. homesickness etc.

2 Some = v. practical e.g. *arranging accommodation*
   Brit. way of life e.g. *strange environment,*
                    social habits
3 Little practice *using Eng.*
   When 1st speak to Eng. person = *shock*
   Great diff. *in understanding*
Reasons: (i) Eng. people *speak v. quickly*
          (ii)   ,,   ,,   ,, *with variety of accents*
          (iii) Different styles (speech) *in*
                 different situations

What can student do?
    (a) *Attend Eng. classes* & lang. lab.
    (b) *Listen to radio & TV*
    (c) Most imp. = *meet Eng. people*
Prob. diff. in *speaking Eng. fluently*
   Advice: 1 *simplify lang., e.g. short sentences*
            2 try to *think in Eng.* NOT *translate*
            3 practise *speaking as much as poss.*
            4 *Eng. structure — educated use — imitate*

Abbreviations used above:

poss.	= possible	imp.	= important
v.	= very	prob.	= probable
Brit.	= British	e.g.	= for example
1st	= first	*sts.*	= *students*
Eng.	= English	*lang.*	= *language*
diff.	= difficulty	*poss.*	= *possible*
lang. lab.	= language laboratory	*probs.*	= *problems*

Unit 1   Stage 3   Text

SOME OF THE PROBLEMS FACING LEARNERS OF ENGLISH

Today I'd like to talk about some of the problems that students face when they follow a course of study through the medium of English—if English is not their mother tongue. The purpose is to show that we're aware of students' problems, and that by analysing them perhaps it'll be possible to suggest how some of them may be
5   overcome.

    The problems can be divided into three broad categories: psychological, cultural and linguistic. The first two categories mainly concern those who come to study in Britain. I'll comment only briefly on these first two and then spend most of the time looking at linguistic difficulties which apply to everyone wherever they are learning
10   English. Some of the common psychological problems really involve fear of the unknown: for example, whether one's academic studies will be too difficult, whether one will fail the examinations, etc. All students share these apprehensions. It's probably best for a student not to look too far ahead but to concentrate day-by-day on increasing his knowledge and developing his ability. The overseas student in
15   Britain may also suffer from separation from his family and possible homesickness; enjoyment of his activities in Britain and the passage of time are the only real help here.

Looking now at the cultural problems, we can see that some of them are of a very practical nature, e.g. arranging satisfactory accommodation; getting used to British money (or the lack of it!), British food and weather (neither is always bad!). Some of the cultural difficulties are less easy to define: they are bound up with the whole range of alien customs, habits and traditions—in other words, the British way of life. Such difficulties include: settling into a strange environment and a new academic routine; learning a new set of social habits, ranging from the times of meals to the meanings of gestures; expressing appropriate greetings; understanding a different kind of humour; and learning how to make friends. Being open-minded and adaptable is the best approach to some of the difficulties listed here.

The largest category is probably linguistic. Let's look at this in some detail.

Most students will have learnt English at school, but if they've already been to college or university in their own countries they'll have studied mostly in their own language except, perhaps, for reading some textbooks and journals in English. In other words, they'll have had little everyday opportunity to practise using English.

When foreign learners first have the opportunity to speak to an English-speaking person they may have a shock: they often have great difficulty in understanding! There are a number of reasons for this. I'll just mention three of them.

Firstly, it seems to students that English people speak very quickly. Secondly, they speak with a variety of accents. Thirdly, different styles of speech are used in different situations, e.g. everyday spoken English, which is colloquial and idiomatic, is different from the English used for academic purposes. For all of these reasons students will have difficulty, mainly because they lack practice in listening to English people speaking English. Don't forget, by the way, that if students have difficulty in understanding English-speaking people, these people may also have difficulty in understanding the students!

What can a student do then to overcome these difficulties? Well, obviously, he can benefit from attending English classes and if a language laboratory is available use it as much as possible. He should also listen to programmes in English on the radio and TV. Perhaps most important of all, he should take every available opportunity to meet and speak with native English-speaking people. He should be aware, however, that English people are, by temperament, often reserved and may be unwilling to start a conversation. Nevertheless, if he has the courage to take the initiative, however difficult it may seem to be, most English people will respond. He will need patience and perseverance!

In addition to these problems regarding listening and understanding, the student probably has difficulty in speaking English fluently. He has the *ideas*, he knows *what* to say (in his own language) but he doesn't know *how* to say it *in English*. The advice here will seem difficult to follow but it's necessary. Firstly, he must simplify his language so that he can express himself reasonably clearly; for example, short sentences will be better than long ones. Secondly, he must try to *think* in English, not translate from his mother tongue. This'll only begin to take place when his use of English becomes automatic; using a language laboratory and listening to as much English as possible will help. In general, he should practise speaking as much as possible. He should also notice the kind of English, and its structure, that educated people use, and try to imitate it.

Other difficulties that the student may have, e.g. note-taking, writing, reading, etc., will be dealt with in other talks.

Unit 2   Stage 1   Text

LISTENING AND UNDERSTANDING

1 A student learning English often finds the following problems when he listens to
2 talks or lectures:
3   Firstly, he doesn't identify all the words correctly.
4   Secondly, he finds it difficult to remember what was said.
5   Thirdly, he can't always follow the argument.
6 There are other problems too, such as understanding different accents.

Unit 2   Stage 1   Notes

(Figures in brackets refer to line numbers above.)

1 *PRONUNCIATION*
   (a) *weak forms and contractions*
       (1) A /ə/ ; the /ðə/ ; he /hɪ/
       (1) to /tə/
       (3) doesn't /dʌznt/ ; the /ðə/
       (5) can't /kɑnt/ ; the /ðɪ/
       (6) there are /ðərə/ ; as /əz/

   (b) *plurals*   /s/z/
       talks
       accents   } /s/
       finds
       problems
       listens   } /z/
       lectures
       words

2 *STRUCTURES*
   (a) adverbs of frequency: immediately before the principal verb (or 'stem'):
       (1) (he) often finds
       (5) he can't always follow
   (b) find + it + adjective + to do something
       (4) he finds it difficult to remember

3 *VOCABULARY*
   (1) to listen to
   (5) follow the argument (= *understand*)
   (6) such as (= e.g., for example)

Unit 2   Stage 2   Key to the Exercises

(Figures in brackets refer to line numbers in the Text in Exercise 2, located in the
front section of the book.)

Exercise 1
1 F   (3–4)
2 T   (9–12)
3 F   (13) and (15–18)
4 F   (19–21)
5 T   (29–30)

Exercise 2
(1) often finds   (2) he listens   (3) doesn't always   (4) i.e.   (6) there are

101

(7) finishes   (9) fails   (10) weak   (11) sometimes   (13) what's been
(14) be studied   (15–16) they've been   (17) There's   (19) argument   (21) for this
(22) don't   (26) lecturers   (27) which are   (28) uses   (29) formal

Exercise 3

1   F   In speech, however, it's very difficult to decide where one word finishes and the next one begins. (6–7)
2   T   In writing, all the letters are easy to identify. In speech, many of the sounds cause a student difficulty and he fails to identify them. (7–9)
3   T   The listener has to concentrate very hard, therefore, on identifying and understanding them *immediately*. (16–17)
4   F   .... because they're concentrating on taking notes, they may *miss* developments in the argument. (23–24)
5   T   .... students have difficulty understanding different accents.... it's usually the vowels which are pronounced differently. (25–27)

Exercise 4

(a)   (1) meets   (2) listens   (3) finishes   (4) starts   (5) cause   (6) fails   (7) occur   (8) have   (9) identifies   (10) do   (11) arises   (12) uses   (13) pronounces   (14) takes   (15) speaks

(b)

/s/	/z/	/ɪz/
meets	listens	finishes
starts	fails	arises
takes	identifies	uses
speaks		pronounces

Exercise 5

(a)   The students also *sometimes* find it difficult to hear the unstressed syllable in a word. (11–12)
(b)   A more formal style can *generally* be followed more easily than a colloquial one. (29–30)
(c)   1 .... can *often* etc. be ....
      2 .... may *frequently* etc. be misunderstood
      3 .... *rarely* etc. repeats ....
      4 .... must *always* understand ....
      5 .... may *sometimes* fail ....
      6 .... *never* causes ....
      7 .... will *generally* be followed ....
Note: it is sometimes possible for the adverb to be placed in a different position if a different degree of emphasis is required (e.g. see Unit 3, Exercise 5).

Unit 2   Stage 3   Guided Note-taking

Suggested notes, completed in italic type.

Title: *Listening & understanding*

Probs.:

1   Doesn't identify *all words, i.e. known words*

Reasons: (i) in speech 1 word *runs into next*
           (ii) *vowels & consonants*   = v. diff.
                to identify
           (iii) Some words pronounced *with weak form*
                e.g. '*there are*'
                unstressed syllables   e.g. <u>cotton</u>, <u>carbon</u>

2 Remembering *what's been said*
   In listening got to *follow speed of speaker*
   Concentrate on *identifying & understanding*
   In for. lang. brain *has too much to do*
   In own lang. *can even predict words*

3 Can't follow *argument*   (partly due to *1st 2 diffs.*   )
   <u>Why?</u>   (1)   don't recognize *signals = points are imp.*
               (2)   try too hard to *understand everything*
               (3)   *must concentrate on taking notes*

<u>Other probs.</u>:
   (a)   <u>Pron.</u> of Eng. changes *from 1 country to another*
         & from *region to region*   e.g. *bus, love, mum*
         N.B. usually vowels *have variants*
   (b)   <u>Style</u> of Eng. — v. formal — or *colloquial/slang*
                        more formal = *easier to understand*
   (c)   <u>Also</u>: *speed of lecture*
         common use of irony
         Eng. humour   etc.

New abbreviations used above:

diff.	= difficult	pron. = pronunciation
for.	= foreign	N.B. = note
		diffs. = *difficulties*
		i.e. = *that is to say*

Unit 2   Stage 3   Text

LISTENING AND UNDERSTANDING

A student learning English often finds <u>the following</u> problems when he listens to talks or lectures.

<u>Firstly</u>, he doesn't always identify all the words correctly. I refer here to known words, i.e. words which the student would certainly recognize in print. <u>Let's examine</u>
5   <u>some of</u> the reasons for this particular difficulty. In writing, there are clear spaces between each word; in speech, one word runs into the next. It's very difficult to decide, therefore, where one word finishes and the next one begins.

In writing, the words consist of letters of the alphabet. These letters have a fixed shape: they're easy to identify. In speech, however, vowel and consonant sounds
10   are often very difficult to identify. Some of these sounds may not exist in the student's native language. Many of them, particularly the vowel sounds, are given different pronunciations by different English speakers.

<u>Finally</u>, some words in English, words like 'and' or 'there' or 'are' or 'will' are

frequently pronounced with their weak or reduced form in speech. This is sometimes
so short that non-native speakers, perhaps not accustomed to it, fail to recognize
it at all. Many students, for example, don't recognize the normal pronunciation
/ðərə/ for the words 'there are' which occur at the beginning of so many English
sentences. Furthermore, they encounter a similar problem with unstressed syllables
which are part of a longer word. For instance, think of the word 'cotton', which is
spelt 'c-o-t-t-o-n'. I'll repeat that: 'c-o-t-t-o-n'. Each letter is the same size; no
difference is made between the first syllable 'cot-' and the second syllable '-ton'. In
speech, however, the first syllable is stressed, the second is unstressed. The word is
not pronounced 'cot-ton' but 'COT n'. The same is true for the word 'carbon', spelt
'c-a-r-b-o-n'; it's not pronounced 'car-bon' but 'CAR bn'

But I want now to come on to the second main problem: the difficulty of
remembering what's been said. Again, the problem here is much less difficult in the
written rather than the spoken form. Words on a page are permanently fixed in
space. They don't disappear like words that are spoken. They remain in front of
you. You can choose your own speed to read them whereas in listening you've got
to follow the speed of the speaker. A difficult word, or sentence, on the printed
page can be read again, whereas a word not clearly heard is rarely repeated. The
listener, therefore, finds that he has to concentrate so hard on identifying the words
correctly and on understanding them that he has little time left to remember.

In a foreign language his brain simply has too much to do. In his own language,
of course, he's able not only to identify and understand the words automatically but
also he can often even predict the words which are going to come. His brain, therefore,
has much more time to remember.

Thirdly, I want to deal with a problem that worries most students in a lecture.
The problem is this—they can't always follow the argument. This is, of course, partly
due to the first two difficulties I've discussed. When you have difficulty in identifying
or remembering words and sentences, you obviously won't be able to follow the
argument. But even those students who can do these two things perfectly well have
problems in following a quite straightforward argument. Why is this? I'll suggest
three reasons here. Firstly, students don't always recognize the signals which tell the
listener that certain points are important. Some of these signals will be quite different
from those employed in writing. Secondly, some students try too hard to understand
everything. When they come to a small but difficult point, they waste time trying to
work it out, and so they may miss a more important point. Thirdly, students must
concentrate very hard on taking notes and therefore may miss developments in the
argument. But note-taking is a separate subject which will be dealt with in a later
talk.

There are, however, other problems the student is faced with, which I'd like to
mention briefly.

It's always a surprise to students to discover how much the pronunciation of
English changes from one English-speaking country to another, and from region to
region. Many lecturers from Britain have a B.B.C.-type accent, the type of English
associated mainly with the South of England and most commonly taught to non-
native speakers. However, other lecturers will speak differently. To give an example
/bʌs/, /lʌv/, /mʌm/ etc., as spoken in the south, are pronounced in Manchester and
many other parts as /bʊs/, /lʊv/ and /mʊm/. Southern English /grɑs/, /fɑst/, /pɑθ/
are pronounced in Yorkshire and elsewhere as /græs/, /fæst/ and /pæθ/. It's worth
noticing that it's usually the vowels which have variants, though sometimes it may
be the consonants. For instance, a Scotsman will roll his 'r's', whereas a Londoner

won't. So a lecturer with a particularly strong regional accent will cause non-native speakers considerable difficulty.

Whether a student follows a lecture easily or not depends also on the style of English the lecturer uses. By 'style' I mean the *type* of English chosen to express an idea: at one extreme it may be very formal, at the other colloquial or even slang. Generally speaking, the more formal the style, the easier it is for the student to understand. For example, a lecturer who says, formally, 'This is undoubtedly the writer's central point' will be readily understood. On the other hand if he says, 'That's really what the writer's on about', many students will have difficulty in understanding.

Other factors, which I haven't the time to discuss in detail, may also be involved. These include the speed at which the lecture is delivered, the rather common use of irony, the peculiarly English sense of humour, references which presuppose a knowledge of British culture, etc.

All these factors combine to make it a formidable task for students to follow lectures comfortably. It's clearly helpful to be aware of the problems and to get as much practice as possible in listening to and trying to understand spoken English.

Unit 3   Stage 1   Text

LECTURES AND NOTE-TAKING

1 When a student takes notes in a lecture, he has to do four things:
2   Firstly, he has to understand what's said, as the speaker says it.
3   Secondly, he has to decide which points are most important.
4   Thirdly, he has to write these points down.
5   Fourthly, he has to show how these points are connected.

Unit 3   Stage 1   Notes

(Figures in brackets refer to line numbers above.)

1   *PRONUNCIATION*
In the following words notice the *syllables* that carry the *main stress* (underlined):

student (1)   important (3)   understand (2)

                      connected (5)   decide   (3)

Note also, where there is an unstressed syllable at the end of words such as 'student' and 'important' the /n/ often 'takes the place of' the vowel, which is not pronounced, e.g.

/stjudn̩t/   /ɪmpɔtn̩t/

Non-native students of English often pronounce and, therefore, expect to hear, a full vowel in such words (see examples given in Unit 2 Stage 3 Text). Because of this, the normal pronunciation:

/brɪtn̩/ may not always be recognized as 'Britain'
/fraɪtn̩/ may not always be recognized as 'frighten'
/hɪdn̩/ may not always be recognized as 'hidden'
/ɔtnt/ may not always be recognized as 'oughtn't'.

105

2 *STRUCTURE*
   have to do something: express obligation or necessity
   (1) he has to do .... (also in lines 2–5)

3 *VOCABULARY*
   (2) as the speaker says it (= at the same time as ....)
   (4) to write something down (= to put down on paper, i.e. to make a note of something)

Unit 3   Stage 2   Key to the Exercises

(Figures in brackets refer to line numbers in the Text in Exercise 2, located in the front section of the book.)

Exercise 1
1 T (2)
2 F (5–6)
3 F (14–16)
4 F (19–20)
5 T (22–24)

Exercise 2
(1) has to (2) what's said (3) can't (4) pattern (6) this (7) says (9) such as
(9) this is (11) they're (12) indirect (12) he'll (14) that faces (15) deciding
(17) should (19) ought (19) to choose (20) isn't (22) he's (23) signs
(24) he'll be able

Exercise 3
1 T He can't stop the lecture in order to look up a new word .... (2–3)
2 F .... use a more colloquial style. A sentence such as 'This is the crunch' ....
       will often cause difficulty .... (8–10)
3 F .... these indirect signals .... (12)
4 T .... the important information words (usually nouns, ...) (17–18)
5 T .... he'll be able to understand the framework of the lecture more easily ....
       (24)
       notes must show the connections between the various points he's noted.
       (21–22)

Exercise 4
(a) (i) he will find it difficult to decide what's important. (12–13)
     (ii) he will be able to understand the framework of the lecture more easily. (24)
(b) suggestions given; other answers are possible:
     2 you should practise speaking as much as possible.
     3 you must sit nearer the front.
     4 you should listen to the radio and TV.
     5 If you have difficulty finding a book.
     6 If you want to meet a lot of students.
     7 If you want to find (or rent) a flat.

Exercise 5

1	is	—	what/said	9	use	—	however,/a
2	in	—	lecture/order	10	such	—	sentence/as
3	an	—	check/unfamiliar	11	is	—	this/the
4	has	—	student/to	12	cause	—	often/difficulty
5	is (or: 's)	—	what/important	13	they	—	when/are
6	do	—	may/this	14	If	—	point./the
7	says	—	he/'this	15	it	—	find/difficult.
8	will	—	student/have				

Unit 3   Stage 3   Guided Note-taking

Suggested notes, completed in italic type.

Title: *Lectures & note-taking*

4 most *imp. skills*   :

   1   <u>Understand what lecturer says</u> *as he says it*

      cannot *stop to look up new words*

      Often poss. to understand much by *concentrating*

         on points = most imp.

   2   What's imp.?

      Most imp. info. = *title*   make sure *write it down*

                   implies *major points*

        Good lecturer *signals what's imp.*

                direct   or *indirect*   signals

          Explicit = write it down!

          Indirect = *pause*   or *speak slowly*   etc.

                = sth. imp.

                quickly? softly? short pauses etc.

                = sth. incidental

   3   <u>Main points: write them down</u> — has to do *quickly & clearly*

         (i) helps to *abbreviate*

         (ii) select only words → *max. info. = nouns*

         (iii) writing only *1 point each line*

      Diff. in *finding time to write* —

          connectives   may guide:

        (a)   in same direction = *safe to write*

                    e.g. *moreover*

        (b)   'however' etc. = *new info.* ∴ *listen*

   4   <u>Show *connections between points* by</u>

      visual presentation:

      e.g. use of *spacing, underlining*   etc.

      points should *be numbered*

New abbreviations used above

info. = information   *max. = maximum*

sth. = something

Unit 3 Stage 3 Text

LECTURES AND NOTE-TAKING

Note-taking is a complex activity which requires a high level of ability in many separate skills. To-day I'm going to analyse the four most important of these skills.

Firstly, the student has to understand what the lecturer says *as he says it*. The student cannot stop the lecture in order to look up a new word or check an unfamiliar sentence pattern. This puts the *non-native speaker* of English under a particularly severe strain. Often—as we've already seen in a previous lecture— he may not be able to recognize words in speech which he understands straightaway in print. He'll also meet words in a lecture which are completely new to him. While he should, of course, try to develop the ability to infer their meaning from the context, he won't always be able to do this successfully. He must not allow failure of this kind to discourage him however. It's often possible to understand much of a lecture by concentrating solely on those points which are most important. But how does the student decide what's important? This is in itself another skill he must try to develop. It is, in fact, the second of the four skills I want to talk about to-day.

Probably the most important piece of information in a lecture is the title itself. If this is printed (or referred to) beforehand the student should study it carefully and make sure he's in no doubt about its meaning. Whatever happens he should make sure that he writes it down accurately and completely. A title often implies many of the major points that will later be covered in the lecture itself. It should help the student therefore to decide what the main point of the lecture will be.

A good lecturer, of course, often signals what's important or unimportant. He may give direct signals or indirect signals. Many lecturers, for example, explicitly tell their audience that a point is important and that the student should write it down. Unfortunately, the lecturer who's trying to establish a friendly relationship with his audience is likely on these occasions to employ a colloquial style. He might say such things as 'This is, of course, the crunch' or 'Perhaps you'd like to get it down'. Although this will help the student who's a native English-speaker, it may very well cause difficulty for the non-native English speaker. He'll therefore have to make a big effort to get used to the various styles of his lecturers.

It's worth remembering that most lecturers also give *indirect* signals to indicate what's important. They either pause or speak slowly or speak loudly or use a greater range of intonation, or they employ a combination of these devices, when they say something important. Conversely, their sentences are delivered quickly, softly, within a narrow range of intonation and with short or infrequent pauses when they are saying something which is incidental. It is, of course, helpful for the student to be aware of this and for him to focus his attention accordingly.

Having sorted out the main points, however, the student still has to write them down. And he has to do this quickly and clearly. This is, in fact, the third basic skill he must learn to develop. In order to write at speed most students find it helps to abbreviate. They also try to select only those words which give maximum information. These are usually nouns, but sometimes verbs or adjectives. Writing only one point on each line also helps the student to understand his notes when he comes to read them later. An important difficulty is, of course, finding time to write the notes. If the student chooses the wrong moment to write he may miss a point of greater importance. Connecting words or connectives may guide him to a correct choice here. Those connectives which indicate that the argument is proceeding in the same direction also tell the listener that it's a safe time to write. 'Moreover',

'furthermore', 'also', etc., are examples of this. Connectives such as 'however', 'on the other hand' or 'nevertheless' usually mean that new and perhaps unexpected
50 information is going to follow. Therefore, it may, on these occasions, be more appropriate to listen.

The fourth skill that the student must develop is one that is frequently neglected. He must learn to show the connections between the various points he's noted. This can often be done more effectively by a visual presentation than by a lengthy state-
55 ment in words. Thus the use of spacing, of underlining, and of conventional symbols plays an important part in efficient note-taking. Points should be numbered, too, wherever possible. In this way the student can see at a glance the framework of the lecture.

Unit 4   Stage 1   Text

ATTITUDES TOWARDS THE LEARNING OF VOCABULARY

1 Learners of English often hold the following views on the subject of vocabulary.
2   Firstly, they think that nearly every word in English has one meaning.
3   Secondly, they think that every word has an exact translational equivalent.
4   Thirdly, they think that as soon as they know the meaning of a word, they're in
5 a position to use it correctly.

Unit 4   Stage 1   Notes

(Figures in brackets refer to line numbers above.)

1 *PRONUNCIATION*
   (a) hold the   (1)⎫
        think that (4)⎭
        Not all final consonant sounds are *fully* pronounced, e.g. /d/ and /k/ at the end of 'hold' and 'think' are not 'exploded' because of the effect of the following sound.
   (b) Notice the *syllable* that carries the *main stress* in the following:
            translation → translational
            occupation → occupational
            tradition   → traditional

2 *STRUCTURE*
   (a) (2, 3, 4) they think that ....
        The object of 'think' is a 'that'—clause; 'that' is often omitted, especially in informal speech.
   (b) (3) every word has .... ⎫ same meaning, different grammatical
            all the words have ....⎭ construction

3 *VOCABULARY*
   (1) to hold .... views (= to have opinions)
   (2) *nearly* every word (=almost/practically: 2 very common alternatives)
   (5) to be in a position to .... (= to be able to ....)

Unit 4 Stage 2 Key to the Exercises

(Figures in brackets refer to line numbers in the Text in Exercise 2, located in the front section of the book.)

Exercise 1
1 F (1–2)
2 F (4–7)
3 T (8, 11–14)
4 F (16–17)
5 T (23–28)

Exercise 2
(1) research (2) towards (3) I'll mention (4) has (7) for quite (8) these
(9) that they're (10) their (11) were taught (12) learned (or: learnt)
(15) emerged (19) other (19) won't (21) principle (23) another
(25) untrue (27) as well as (28) be used (29) one's (30) repetition.

Exercise 3
1 F ....the attitudes of postgraduate science students.... The results were surprising. (1–3)
2 F *One* reason may be that they're all science students.... *Another* reason, of course, could be the way in which these students were taught. (8–11)
3 F *Sometimes* one word in English can only be translated by a phrase.... (17–18)
4 T Translation machines, which tried to work on this principle (i.e. a one word for one word translation process) failed completely. (20–22)
5 F ....these students made such a mistake (8)....They have used vocabulary lists (etc.) (12–14)....the best way to increase one's vocabulary....observation, imitation and repetition. (29–30)

Exercise 4
(a) 1 far from the truth (line 17)
     2 completely false (20–21)
     3 another error (23)
     4 untrue (25)
     5 particularly false (26)
(b) (ii) (B2) It's *probably* best for a student to concentrate on developing his ability.
     (iii) (C1) A student who studies abroad *may* (or: *can*) suffer from homesickness in the early stages.
     (iv) (A1) English people *seem to* speak very quickly.
     (v) (C2) *Perhaps* watching TV is* the activity that will* help to develop listening comprehension* the most.
          Note: * *perhaps* may be placed in these positions instead.
          possibly may be used in the same positions.

Exercise 5
(a) 1 glance: 2
     2 then: 3
     3 emerge: 2
     4 practically: 3
     5 principle: 1
(b) *n.* = noun
     adv. = adverb

110

vi. = verb intransitive (i.e. used without a direct object)
[*c.*] = countable noun

Unit 4   Stage 3   Guided Note-taking

Suggested notes, completed in italic type.

<u>Title</u>: *Attitudes towards learning vocab.*

<u>Misconceptions</u>:

1 Every Eng. word = *1 meaning*
   <u>Majority</u> = *more than 1*
   How arrived at false conclusion?
      (i) *science students*
      (ii) *way st's taught Eng. — vocab. lists*

2 Every word in Eng. = *exact translational equivalent*   NO!
   S'times no equivalent: may employ *phrase*
   1 word in st's. lang. = *1 of 2 poss. words in Eng.*
                        e.g. *do & make*
   Translation = *diff. to do well*
                 can't be done *by matching single words*

3 Word can be used correctly *as soon as meaning known*   NO!
   Eng. = *larger vocab. & rich in synonyms*
            e.g. starts, & commences   (=formal)
   More imp. = *grammatical matter*
            e.g. *make & do*

Best way to *increase vocab.*   :
      (1) *observation*
      (2) *imitation*
      (3) *repetition*

New abbreviations used above:

univ. = university	st's = student's
s'times = sometimes	*vocab.* = *vocabulary*

Unit 4   Stage 3   Text

ATTITUDES TOWARDS THE LEARNING OF VOCABULARY

A recent university research project into the attitudes of non-native English-speaking postgraduate science students towards the learning of English vocabulary has revealed some surprising results. <u>Among the many</u> misconceptions, <u>the following</u> were perhaps <u>the most serious.</u>

5   <u>Firstly,</u> most of the subjects of the enquiry think that nearly every word in English has just one meaning. While it's true, of course, that many words in English do have only one meaning, it can easily be shown that the majority have more than one. It's not uncommon, for example, to find seven or eight meanings listed for quite 'simple' words. A superficial glance at any respectable English dictionary will
10   demonstrate this quite clearly.
       One wonders how, then, these students have arrived at such a false conclusion.

One reason, of course, may be that they're science students. Scientific terms generally possess only one, precisely defined, meaning. It is, in fact, exactly this quality that makes these words distinctive in English, or indeed in any other language. Another reason could be the way in which these students were taught English. For example, long vocabulary lists are still an important feature in the foreign language learning programmes of many countries. On one side of the page is the word in English; on the other side a single word in the student's native language.

But this brings me on to the second major misconception. Practically all the students think that every word in English has an exact translational equivalent in their own language. Again this is a gross distortion of the truth. Sometimes a *word* in the student's native language may not have an equivalent in English at all, which may have to employ a *phrase* as a translation. Sometimes one word in the student's language may be translated by one of two possible words in English. The difficulty that many students have with the two verbs 'do' and 'make' is an example of this. Often the area of meaning covered by one word in the student's language may be wider or narrower than the area of meaning covered by a corresponding word in English. This sometimes happens with the naming of colours, where most students would expect an exact correspondence between their language and English. The borders between the primary colours of the spectrum are, however, drawn at different places in different languages. Translation, in fact, is a particularly difficult thing to do well. It certainly can't be done by matching single words from one language with single words from another. At first, those computer scientists who attempted to construct an automatic translation machine made this mistake. The machines often produced nonsense.

The third important misconception on the part of the students is their idea that a word can be used correctly as soon as its meaning is known. This is untrue for any language but is perhaps particularly false for English. English has a larger vocabulary than any other language. The reason for this, of course, is that it has been influenced by several other languages. It has, in fact, borrowed words from many sources. It is, therefore, particularly rich in synonyms. The students will often find that English speakers use Anglo-Saxon words in their everyday spoken language, but prefer a Latin synonym for formal written language. Thus, while an English speaker will say 'Term starts on the third of October', he'll often write (particularly in an official notice) 'Term commences on the third of October'. If the foreign student, having learned the word 'commence', uses it in ordinary conversation, his English will sound unusually formal. This is, of course, a matter of style. Perhaps more important is a grammatical matter, namely that some words which mean the same can only be used when certain other words are present. A simple example will illustrate this. The verbs 'make' and 'do' cover roughly the same area of meaning in English. You cannot, however, say 'I'll make my homework', you must say 'I'll do my homework'. On the other hand, you must say 'I'll make a cup of coffee', not 'I'll do a cup of coffee'.

What, then, is the best way to increase one's vocabulary in a foreign language? This can be answered in three words. Firstly, observation: the unknown word should be observed in its context: in other words, the neighbouring words and the grammatical construction should be noted. A good dictionary should be referred to, and examples of the usage of the word should be noted. Secondly, imitation: the student should use the new word in appropriate contexts, imitating the examples he has noted. Finally, repetition: he'll need to practise using the word several times before he's confident that he can use it correctly; in other words, repetition is necessary if the new word is to 'stick', and especially if it is to enter the student's *active* vocabulary.

Unit 5   Stage 1   Text

EFFECTIVE READING

1 Many students when they read have no particular purpose in mind. They can make
2 their reading more effective by making use of a plan.
3   Firstly, they should decide precisely *why* they're reading the book. Then they
4 should decide exactly *what* they're going to read. It's useful to get a general idea
5 of the contents before starting to read. Students should then ask themselves a specific
6 question about their reading. Finally, they should try to answer it by making notes
7 as they read.

Unit 5   Stage 1   Notes

(Figures in brackets refer to line numbers above.)

1 *PRONUNCIATION*
   (a) The *sounds* /i/ as in 'read' and /ɪ/ as in 'it' are often confused. Practise them
       in both listening and speaking, making sure there is a contrast: read it; read
       it please.
   (b) Notice which *syllable* carries the main stress in the following words:

      particular (1)   effective (2)   precisely (3)   exactly (4)   specific (5)

   Note also vowel reduction in the syllable preceding the stressed syllable:
   e.g. in 'particular', 'par' is pronounced /pə/ not /pɑ/.
   (c) Some *words* in a sentence have a stronger stress than others. Notice in the
       Text that *why* and *what* have an *extra* strong stress. If the strong stress is
       changed it can give a different emphasis to the sentence. Practise changing
       the *extra* strong stress in:

   they're reading the book (i.e. not the other people)

   they're reading the book (i.e. not discussing it)

   they're reading the book (i.e. not the newspaper)

2 *STRUCTURE*
   (a) possessive adjective + verb stem + ing
       (2) and (6) *their reading*
   (b) preposition + verb stem + ing
       (2) and (6) *by making*
       (5) *before starting*
   (c) have *no* particular purpose: 'no' negates the noun 'purpose'
       cf. have *not any* particular purpose: 'not' negates the verb 'have' and requires
       'any' or 'a' before the following noun.

3 *VOCABULARY*
   (1) have .... in mind (= think about)

Unit 5   Stage 2   Key to the Exercises

(Figures in brackets refer to line numbers in the Text in Exercise 2, located in the front section of the book.)

Exercise 1

1 F (7–8)
2 T (9–13)
3 F (14–17)
4 F (19–21)
5 F (24–26)

Exercise 2

(1) recommends   (2) invaluable   (3) refer to   (5) tend to   (7) don't have
(8) they're   (9) much more   (11) it's to   (12) exactly   (14–15) This can be
(16) in order to   (18) their   (20) them to   (21) can be read   (21) the most
(23) that's been   (24) must   (26) as   (27) both   (27) detailed

Exercise 3

1 F The teacher *may* just refer to a few pages and not the whole book. (3–4)
2 T (*By implication.*) *Unfortunately*, when many students pick up a book to read they tend to have *no* particular purpose in mind. (5–6)
3 F ....students should ask *themselves* a specific question about their reading. They should then try to answer it by making notes as they read.... This is, perhaps, the most effective part of the reading strategy. (18–22)
4 T If a student puts into practice everything that's been suggested so far, can we say that he reads efficiently? Well.... it's important that a student reads as quickly as possible. (23–26)
5 F ....his slowest speed, which is for detailed study (his fastest is for getting a general idea). (27–28)

Exercise 4

(a) Suggested answers:
   1 louder/quieter/softer etc.....than....
   2 lower....than....
   3 faster/quicker....than....
   4 faster/better than....
(b) 1 more difficult....than....
   2 more practical....than....
   3 more serious than....
   4 more seriously....than....
(c) 1 A B.A. degree is not as specialized as an M.A.
   2 An arts degree course is not as long as a medical degree course.
   3 A student's health is as important as his academic ability.
   4 Multiple-choice questions are not as difficult as essay-type questions.

NOTE ON COMPARISONS

1 Some common two-syllable adjectives, e.g. common, handsome, polite, quiet, can have either type of comparison:

common { commoner / more common } { commonest / most common }

2 A small group of very frequent adjectives have irregular comparison:

bad	worse	worst
far	further/farther	furthest/farthest
good	better	best
many	more	most

3 A small group of adverbs have irregular comparison:

badly	worse	worst
far	further/farther	furthest/farthest
little	less	least
much	more	most
well	better	best

Exercise 5

(a) 1 c   (b) 1 Admittedly
    2 b   2 Theoretically
    3 a   3 Naturally
    4 b   4 Superficially
                       5 Actually

NOTE. Some common *comment adverbials* are given below.

Admittedly	In fact	Officially	Basically	Fortunately
Certainly	Actually	Superficially	Fundamentally	Hopefully
Definitely	Really	Technically	Logically	Luckily
Indeed		Theoretically		Naturally
Surely				Preferably
				Strangely
				Surprisingly
				Unexpectedly
				Unfortunately

Unit 5   Stage 3   Guided Note-taking

Suggested notes, completed in italic type.

Title: *Effective reading*
      When lecturer recommends book = for *part. purpose*
        not *whole book*   — just *few pp.*
      When sts. read = *no part. purpose*
        Sts. often read *p. by p. etc., i.e. slowly*
        Result = (1)   no *overall view*
                   (2)   *forget soon*

Reading strategy:
   1 Decide *why reading*
   2   ,,   *what going to read*
        Starting point = *contents p. & index*
   3 Overview of contents: reading *introduction & conclusion*
        Useful to *skim sections & get general idea*
   4 Ask selves *specific Q.*   then A. it *by*
                making notes   : will help them to
                focus on reading & provide summary
                = most *effective element*

e.g. 'Teaching & *Learning in Higher Education*'
— Ruth Beard, *Penguin, 2nd ed., 1972, p. 190*

Increase reading speed *without loss of comprehension*
   3 main reading speeds:
      (i) *slowest = study speed*
      (ii) *average*
      (iii) *fastest = skimming*

Survey — Reading Speeds (— Edward Fry):

Type of reader	Type of reading speed	Speed: words per minute (wpm)	Comprehension per cent (%)
A good reader	Skimming (v. fast)	*800+*	*50%*
	Average	*250–500*	*70%*
	Slow/Study	*200–300*	*80–90%*
A poor reader	Skimming	—	—
	Average	*150–180*	*70%*
	Slow/Study	*90–125*	*80–90%*

Aim at: c. *250 wpm*

New abbreviations used above:

A.   = answer
c.   = about
part. = *particular*

p./pp. = *page/pages*
Q.   = *question*
2nd = *second*
ed.   = *edition*
wpm = *words per minute*

Unit 5   Stage 3   Text

EFFECTIVE READING

When a teacher or lecturer recommends a student to read a book it's usually for a particular purpose. The book may contain useful information about the topic being studied or it may be invaluable for the ideas or views that it puts forward, and so on. In many cases, the teacher doesn't suggest that the *whole* book should be read.
5   In fact, he may just refer to a few pages which have a direct bearing on the matter being discussed.

    Unfortunately, when many students pick up a book to read *they* tend to have no particular purpose in mind other than simply to 'read the book'. Often they open the book and start reading, page by page, line by line, word by word: in other words,
10 slowly and in great detail. The result is that students frequently don't have an

116

overall view of what they're reading; also, they tend to forget fairly soon what they've been reading.

Students can make their reading much more effective by adopting a strategy aimed at helping them to understand and to remember what they read. Firstly, they

15   should decide precisely *why* they're reading the book: perhaps it's to find some information that'll answer a question; perhaps it's to understand a difficult idea or argument, and so on. Then the students should decide exactly *what* they're going to read: it's seldom necessary to read the whole book. A good starting point is the Contents page, at the front of the book; a quick look at the chapter headings may

20   help to indicate what should be read. The Index, at the back of the book, is often extremely useful in helping to pinpoint the exact pages that need to be consulted for *very high degree* particular pieces of information.

When it has been decided what's to be read—a chapter of a book, for example— then it's helpful to get an overview of the contents before starting to read. This can

25   be done by reading the introduction, usually the opening paragraph, and the *take a quick look.* conclusion, usually the final paragraph. In addition, a glance at the headings of sections or sub-sections will show the order in which the items are introduced. As well as doing this, some students find it useful to skim, or read very quickly, some *2 - attempt or effort.* sections in order to get the gist, or general idea, of the contents.

30   Finally, students should ask themselves a specific question connected with the *3 - make sb very tired.* main part of their reading. They should then endeavour to answer it by making appropriate notes as they read. This will help them to focus on the reading as well as providing a summary which can be re-read later. This is, perhaps, the most effective element in the reading strategy.

35   The importance of this last point can be seen from the following quotation taken from *Teaching and Learning in Higher Education,* by Ruth Beard (published by Penguin Books, second edition 1972, page 190). 'One reason for poor comprehension from reading may be that students fail to make notes or to ask themselves questions about the text. Evidence obtained by Carmichael and Dearborn (1948)

40   showed that whereas a reader normally seemed fatigued after one and a half hours, if the reading material was broken down every twenty-five pages by short tests, reminding him what he had read, he could go on without fatigue or loss of efficiency for periods of up to six hours.'

If a student puts into practice everything that's been suggested so far, can we

45   say that he reads efficiently? Well, we must remember that most students have a lot to read and only a limited time in which to read it. As a result, it's important that a student reads as quickly as possible. If he can increase his reading speed without loss of comprehension, then he'll have become a more efficient reader.

Basically, there are three main kinds of silent reading speed, all for different

50   purposes. The slowest speed is *study speed*, for a high level of understanding and when it's necessary to remember details; next is *average speed*, for easier textbooks, novels, etc.; the fastest is *skimming*, when it is not necessary to have a high level of comprehension. Skimming is used to get a general idea of what an article or a book is about.

55   Various surveys have been conducted into students' reading speeds, which are measured by the number of words read in a minute. One, by Edward Fry, showed that a *good reader* achieves 50% comprehension while skimming at more than 800 words a minute; this is, of course, very fast. He has an average speed of about 250–500 words a minute for 70% comprehension. This falls to about 200–300 words

60   a minute for study speed with a high-level comprehension rate of 80–90%. On the

other hand, a *poor reader* is unable to skim at all. The average speed of a poor reader is 150 to 180 words a minute with a comprehension rate of 70%. If 80–90% comprehension is required then the study speed is about 90–125 words a minute.

A reasonable average reading speed for students to aim at is about 250 words a minute.

Unit 6   Stage 1   Text

USING A LIBRARY

1 A student may use a library in various ways. First, he may borrow books from it.
2 Secondly, he may consult reference materials from its shelves. Thirdly, he may use
3 the library for general study purposes. In this lecture, we shall examine aspects of
4 these different activities, with a view to helping the student to use his library more
5 easily and more efficiently.

Unit 6   Stage 1   Notes

(Figures in brackets refer to line numbers above.)

1   *PRONUNCIATION*
   (a) Note the distinction between /v/ and /w/. Many students have great difficulty
      in identifying and pronouncing these sounds accurately.
      (1) in various ways
      (4) with a view to
   (b) Note the pronunciation of

      /'refrəns/—reference
      /'dɪfrənt/—different

   This dropping of the unstressed second syllable is very common in a poly-
   syllabic word stressed on the first syllable. This can cause confusion with
   spelling. Other common examples:

      /'prefrəns/—preference
      /'evrɪ/   —every
      /'sevrəl/   —several
      /'dʒenrəl/ —general
      /'ɪntrəstɪŋ/—interesting

2   *STRUCTURE*
   (a) *Modal:* may use (1, 2), may borrow (1), may consult (2)
         The speaker avoids 'uses', 'borrows', 'consults' as these are too
         definite.
   (b) *Article:* .... may use a library (1)
         .... may use the library (2/3)
         When a countable noun is referred to as an example of a general
         class, it is first preceded by the indefinite article 'a' (as in line 1).
         Later references are then often indicated by 'the' (as in line 3).
   (c) *Purpose:* .... with a view to helping (4)
            This could be expressed by:
               'in order to help'

118

Other occurrences of this rather unusual structure (to + verb stem + ing) are:

'used to doing something'

'look forward to seeing somebody'

Most verbs after 'to' take the infinitive or verb stem form.

3   *VOCABULARY*
(a) *Spelling:* shelf—shelves
         (also half—halves etc.)
         rule: vowel + lf → vowel + lves
(b) (1) various (= different/a number of)
     (1) borrow *from* (compare: lend *to*)
     (3) aspects (= various sides)

Unit 6   Stage 2   Key to the Exercises

(Figures in brackets refer to line numbers in the Text in Exercise 2, located in the front section of the book.)

Exercise 1
1   F   (3–5)
2   T   (6–8)
3   T   (23–24)
4   F   (25–27)
5   T   (29–31)

Exercise 2
(1) various   (2) shelves   (4) a view to   (6) let's have   (7) knows   (8) catalogue
(10) known   (12) pieces of   (14) consists   (15) which appears   (15) lies
(17) Thus   (18) area   (21) encyclopedias   (22) rather than   (23) rare
(25) All these   (28) occasions   (29) simply comes   (30) atmosphere

Exercise 3
1   F   *Thirdly*, he may use the library for general study purposes. (3)
2   T   The card, apart from the author's name, always gives *at least two other* important pieces of information. (11–12)
3   T   It (the call number) normally consists of two parts: the first part, or the class number, which appears on the top line ....; the second part, or the author number, on the next line .... (14–16)
4   F   .... the author number will direct him to the *exact shelf*. (19)
5   F   Finally, professional journals or periodicals are usually kept in the reference section. (24–25)

Exercise 4

(a)

Speaker's aims	Language he uses
(i)	A student may use a library in various ways.
(ii)	First, he may borrow books from it. Secondly, he may consult reference materials from its shelves. Thirdly, he may use the library for general study purposes.
(iii) (a) (b)	In this lecture we shall examine aspects of these activities with a view to helping the student to use his library more easily and more efficiently.

(b) Suggested answers; small variations are possible.

1 A student may use a tape-recorder in various ways. First, he may use it to improve his listening. Secondly, he may use it to practise (his) speaking. Thirdly, he may use it to record lectures. In this talk, we shall examine aspects of these activities with a view to helping the student to use his tape-recorder more easily and more efficiently.

2 A student may use a dictionary in various ways (or: for various reasons). First, he may use it to look up the meaning of new words. Secondly, he may use it to check the spelling of a word. Thirdly, he may use it to see how a word is used. In this talk, we shall examine aspects of these activities with a view to helping the student to use his dictionary more easily and more efficiently.

Exercise 5

1	is	— It/important	12	and	—	imitation/repetition
2	for	— can,/example	13	the	—	in/context
3	more	— much/effective	14	there	—	However,/still
4	help	— will/them	15	is	—	reader/to
5	more	— remember/easily	16	be	—	must/able
6	as	— well/an	17	is	—	who/doing
7	to	— needs/develop	18	to	—	likely/make
8	a	— up/large	19	of	—	contains,/course
9	of	— way/doing	20	journals	—	professional./A
10	an	— Such/idea	21	how	—	know/to
11	to	— contrary/the				

Unit 6   Stage 3   Guided Note-taking

Suggested notes, completed in italic type.

Title: *Using a library*

3 headings: 1 *Borrowing books*
            2 *Consulting ref. mats.*
            3 *Gen. study*

1   Assume *given author & title of book*
    — to borrow from lib.
    — have to *consult author/name catalogue*

Sample Card:

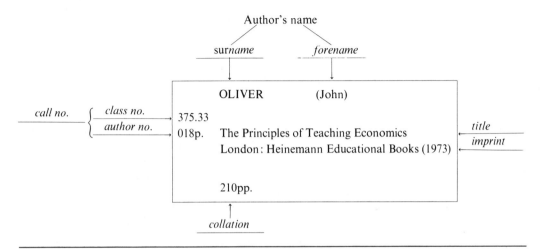

---

2   Ref. section — 3 imp. types of mats.:
        (i) *Books for pieces of info.*   e.g. *dictionaries*
        (ii)   ,,   = *valuable*   e.g. *old ed.*
        (iii) *Prof. journals*
    Encyclopedia gives *overview*
    Dissert./research: need to consult *specialized biblio.*
        v. recent research — *prof. journals*

3   Lib. provides *suitable working environ.*
    Also chat with *fellow sts. in breaks*
    Wise to *set daily targets*
    Q. of *balance & self-discipline*

New abbreviations used above:

lib.   = library   *gen.*   = *general*
ref.   = reference   *no.*   = *number*
mats.   = materials   *prof.*   = *professional*
Dissert. = dissertation   *biblio.* = *bibliography*
                              environ. = *environment*

Unit 6   Stage 3   Text

USING A LIBRARY

The uses a student makes of his college library <u>may be summarized under three broad headings</u>: borrowing books, consulting reference materials and general study. <u>In this lecture we shall examine various aspects of these activities with a view to</u> helping the student to use his library more easily and more efficiently.

5   First of all then, borrowing books. Let's assume a student has been given the
author and title of a certain book which he's been told to read. He wants to *borrow*
it from the library as it'll take some time for him to finish it. As soon as he gets to
the library he should check that the book is in stock, make sure that it's available
for lending, and find out where to locate it on the library shelves. In order to do
10   this he'll have to consult the catalogues. As he has the name of the author, it'll be
easiest to use the author, or name, catalogue. This consists of a list of books entered
on cards in alphabetical order under the name of the author, institution or editor
by which the book is best known. If you look at your hand-out you'll see a sample
card. While I'm talking about this, it might be helpful if you label it in the
15   appropriate places. In this way you'll familiarize yourself with the most important
item in the whole business of using a library.

At the top of the card, then, in the centre, is written the author's name—his
surname always comes first, followed by his forename, also known as 'Christian
name'. The forename is further distinguished from the surname either by punctuation
20   (brackets, or a comma), or by style of printing (the forename is smaller or lighter).

The book's call number, that's to say the number which identifies the book, occurs
near the top left hand corner of the card. This number normally consists of two
parts, each part being printed on a separate line. The first part, on the top line, is
the *class* number, that's to say it's the number which tells you in which subject area
25   the book lies. The Dewey Decimal System, which nearly all libraries use to classify
their books, divides all knowledge up into major subject areas. Every subject has a
number and the number after the decimal point refers to a particular branch of
that subject. The numbers selected range from 000 to 999—but there are an indefinite
number of sub-divisions within these categories. Thus the sample card shows the
30   class number (that's the classification by subject) as 375.33. This number represents
these subdivisions:
300 Social Sciences
370 Education
375 Curriculum
35   375.33 Economics
Beneath this Dewey Decimal number you'll see another number. This is for the
author. The capital letter O represents the first letter of the author's surname. The
following number is especially assigned to this particular name. The small letter which
in some systems follows this number is the first letter of the title of the book. In
40   cataloguing titles, the definite and indefinite article are disregarded. Thus the letter
here is 'p'. While the class number tells the student which general area in the library
to go to in order to find the book, the author number will direct him to the exact
shelf. *document-reciept*

With this information, and having found the book, the student can now fill in the
45   appropriate voucher, or borrowing slip, and have the book date-stamped on the
inside page by the assistant. If the book is already out on loan, then it's usually
possible to reserve it, so that when it's returned the student can be sure of getting it.

That now completes what you need to know about borrowing a book, though
before we move on to consulting reference material, we'll just briefly examine the
50   other details on the name card from the catalogue. Under the author's name, the → *name*
title of the book is printed, followed by the edition. There then appears the *imprint* *address*
details: these give details of publisher, place and date of publication. Finally, under *Publish*
the imprint, you have the *collation* details. These give number of volumes, pages,
illustrations and maps. *examine and compare (two books, manuscripts etc.) in*

122

order to find the differences between them:

55 But now let's look at the second broad use a student may make of his library:
consulting reference material. In addition to the lending section an academic library
always has a reference section. Three important types of materials in this section are:

(1) books which were planned and written to be referred to for *pieces* of information
rather than to be read completely. Examples of such books include dictionaries,
60 bibliographies and encyclopedias.
(2) books which are valuable or difficult to replace. An example would be an old
edition of a book, of which the library has only a single copy, which is out-of-print,
but which is referred to by a regular number of students each year.
(3) professional journals or periodicals.

65 A student who's starting on a new and difficult topic often finds it valuable to
consult an encyclopedia. This type of book is arranged alphabetically by subjects
and it gives an overview of a topic, including definition, description, background
and bibliographical references. The overview is usually clear, concise and authori-
tative. When the student is writing a dissertation or doing a piece of research then
70 he will need to consult a specialized bibliography. This is a book which lists all the
published materials on a particular subject, and in some cases gives a brief summary
of each item. Very recent research, however, may not appear in a bibliography and
the student should, therefore, always consult the relevant professional journals.

On many occasions, however, the student does not come to the library to borrow
75 a book, or even to consult a book from the shelves. He may well come to the library
because it provides a suitable working environment, which is free of charge, spacious,
well-lit and adequately heated. Moreover, he can, if he meets an unexpected problem
in his work, consult one of the reference books or perhaps even a fellow-student.
He can also have a chat with his fellow-students in his breaks. The last point, of
80 course, is often an important one. Many students find their life lonely and demanding,
and they welcome the possibility of social contact. Libraries, of course, have a
'no-talking' rule with the result that these discussions or informal chats normally
take place in a neighbouring coffee bar. There are problems with this, of course.
Students can, if they're not careful, make the library a social centre rather than a
85 study centre. To prevent this, it's wise to set daily targets as regards work. In this
way, one can take any necessary breaks and still complete what has to be finished.
It's all a question of balance and of self-discipline. With a little common-sense, study
can be both efficient and pleasant.

[handwritten margin notes:]
P and pp of light
having or providing much space; roomy.
1 - friendly informal conversation
2 - alone - sad because one lacks friends or companions.
3 - object or mar̲k̲

Unit 7   Stage 1   Text

PROBLEMS OF WRITING IN A FOREIGN LANGUAGE

1 Learners of English usually find that writing is the most difficult skill they have to
2 master. Their errors can be divided into three broad categories:
3   Firstly, errors which lead to a misunderstanding or a breakdown in communication.
4   Secondly, errors which result in ungrammatical English, but which do not interfere
5 with the meaning.
6   Thirdly, errors of style or usage.

Unit 7　Stage 1　Notes

(Figures in brackets refer to line numbers above.)

1　*PRONUNCIATION*
　　'th' = /ð/ in: that, the, they, their, with
　　　　　 = /θ/ in: three, thirdly

　　Note: Many students may, incorrectly, hear and pronounce these sounds as /d/
　　　　and /t/.

2　*STRUCTURE*
　　(a) *Prepositions after verbs*: can be divided into (2), lead to (3), result in (4),
　　　　interfere with (4/5)
　　(b) *Relative clauses*: **with** a relative marker (3 with 'which'); **without** a relative
　　　　　　　　　　　marker ('the most difficult skill . . . they have to master').
　　(c) *Gerund*: i.e. verb stem + ing form used as a noun (e.g. 'writing', line 1). Often
　　　　used when discussing an activity.

3　*VOCABULARY*
　　(1/2) to master = to be proficient at/to gain control over
　　(2)　broad = general
　　(3) error = a more formal word for 'mistake'
　　(3) a misunderstanding = a failure to understand correctly.
　　　　N.B. to misunderstand = to take the wrong meaning
　　　　　　　　not understand = not know the meaning

Unit 7　Stage 2　Key to the Exercises

(Figures in brackets refer to line numbers in the Text in Exercise 2, located in the front section of the book.)

Exercise 1
1　F　(1–2)
2　F　(4–5)
3　T　(10–11)
4　F　(17–18)
5　T　(23–25)

Exercise 2
(2) to master　(3) analyse　(5) They'll　(6) which leads　(7) of these
(8) numerous　(9) tends　(11) This　(11) patterns　(12) which are　(13) choose
(14) too complex　(15) instead of　(16) refers to　(18) interfere　(19) comes into
(20) checks　(23) concerns　(24) he's　(25) they'd

Exercise 3
1　F　Even native speakers of English often find it difficult to write well on their
　　　special subject. (2–3)
2　T　The causes of these misunderstandings and breakdowns are numerous. We
　　　can only try to cover the most important here. (7–9)
3　T　. . . . he may choose to write sentences which are too long and too complex
　　　instead of simpler ones which he can handle more easily. (13–15)

124

4 F The wrong selection of a verb tense often comes into this category .... which doesn't usually interfere with the meaning. (18–19)
5 T When he writes, therefore, he should prepare several drafts. (21–22)

Exercise 4
(a) (i) & (ii)
    2 which are too long and too complex (14)
    3 that the learner of English usually makes (4)
    4 with whom I corresponded
    5 by which the theory was proved
(b) 1 **d**
    2 **c**
    3 **a**
    4 **e**
    5 **b**
(c) 2 The theory *which* (*or: that*) claims all men are equal is very misleading.
    3 The analysis *by which* he tried to prove his theory was very ingenious.
    4 The experiment (*up*)*on which* his theory was based was a complete success.
    5 The report *which* was written later was not convincing.
    6 The survey *from which* the facts were drawn did not cover the whole population.

Exercise 5
(a) 1 accommodation   2 beginning
    3 criticism   4 development
    5 disappeared   6 foreigner
    7 government   8 necessary
    9 occurred   10 writing
   11 interesting   12 studying

(b) 2 attend to — He attends seminars every Monday and Thursday afternoon.
    3 was — Some students were very late.
    4 advices — The tutor gave the student some useful advice.
    5 this means; do — What does this mean? He does not know.
    6 of/social — Psychology is one of the social sciences.
    7 applied/study; no — He applied to study Chemistry, not Physics.
    8 a; during — He had been doing (the, some) research for two years.
    9 have — The student has learned a lot from her lectures.
   10 informations — The information he received was wrong.
   11 /Seems; experiment/a — It seems that the experiment was (*or: is*) a success.
   12 These student should succeeds, if he learn to write accurately the English:
      This student should succeed, if he learns to write English accurately (*or:* These students should succeed, if they learn to write English accurately).

Unit 7   Stage 3   Guided Note-taking

Suggested notes, completed in italic type.

<u>Title</u>: *Probs. of writing in for. lang.*
<u>Writing</u> = *most diff. skill — nat. speaker finds diff.*

Three *main types of error*   :

    1   → misunderstanding or *total breakdown in commun.*
        <u>Causes</u>:
          (i) *use of translation = diff.*
            ∴ try to employ *sentence patterns he knows are correct*
            Eventually *try to think in Eng.*
            Vocab.: *transln. dicts. = make errors prob.*
                — misuse Eng. words *similar form in nat. lang.*
         (ii) Confuse gram. patterns = *sim. in form but differ. in meaning*
            e.g. *used to & to be used to*
        (iii) Sentences = *too long & complex*
            ∴ *organize points before write*
            Rule = *never write sentence more than 3 lines*
        (iv) Sentences = *too short & incomplete*
            e.g. *lack subject or verb*

    2   → irritates & *may mislead*
        e.gs.   1   *wrong verb tense*
              2   concord
              3   *word order*
              4   *article usage*
        ∴ prepare *several drafts*

    3   *stylistic*
        Synonyms = *not always interchangeable*
                 e.g. *terrific & impressive*
                    (*terrific = colloquial*)
        Equally *area & region*

New abbreviations used above:

gram. = grammatical		*nat.*	= *native*
sim. = *similar*		*commun.*	= *communication*
differ. = *different*		*transln.*	= *translation*
org. = *organize*		*dicts.*	= *dictionaries*

Unit 7   Stage 3   Text

PROBLEMS OF WRITING IN A FOREIGN LANGUAGE

Learners of English usually find that writing is the most difficult skill they have to master. The majority of *native* speakers of English have to make an effort to write accurately and effectively even on those subjects which they know very well. The non-native learner, then, is trying to do something that the average native speaker
5   often finds difficult himself.

It may prove helpful, therefore, if I outline the three main types of error the learner of English is likely to make. I'll also try to suggest reasons for these errors and ways of avoiding them.

10 Firstly, and most seriously, there's the type of error which leads to misunderstanding or, even worse, to a total breakdown in communication. The causes of such misunderstandings and breakdowns are numerous, and I'll therefore be able to do no more than try to cover the most important ones here.

Perhaps the most frequent cause of such a breakdown in meaning is the use of translation. Unfortunately translation is a difficult art which can't be performed by 15 a one word to one word matching process. Students, however, often work out a sentence in their own language and then try to translate it in this way. The result is that very often the reader simply cannot understand what the student has written. The individual words, or odd phrases, may make sense but the sentence as a whole makes nonsense. The student should, therefore, always try to employ sentence 20 patterns he knows are correct English. Usually these patterns will be the simple ones he learnt in the earlier stages of his first English course. As he extends his knowledge of the grammar through formal learning, through wide reading and through his contact with native English speakers he'll be able to use a larger number of such sentence patterns. Eventually he should aim to cut out translation altogether. He 25 should, in fact, try to 'think in English'. This is rarely possible in the earlier stages, however.

But it's not only the grammar which suffers when translation is employed. The vocabulary may suffer too. The use of translation dictionaries, unless they are very good and used with extreme care, may make errors more probable. Another factor 30 which is at work here is as follows. Very often those students who come from a language background which is Indo-European, mis-use English words which have a similar form to those in their native language. Spanish speakers, for example, expect the English word 'actually' to mean the same as the Spanish word 'actualmente'. Unfortunately it doesn't.

35 Another very important cause of breakdown in communication in written work is the student's tendency to confuse grammatical patterns which are similar in form but different in meaning. For example 'used to' and 'to be used to'. He may write 'Men are used to believing in their superiority over women' instead of 'Men used to believe in their superiority over women'. Let me repeat the two sentences, 'Men 40 are used to believing in their superiority over women' and 'Men used to believe in their superiority over women'. These two patterns look similar but have completely different meanings.

A third cause is that the student may choose to write sentences which are too long and too complex instead of those simpler ones which he can handle more easily. 45 Many students seem to think that simplicity is suspect. It is, on the contrary, a quality which is much admired in English. Most readers understand that a difficult subject can only be written up 'simply' if the writer understands it very well. A student should, therefore, organize all his points very carefully *before* he starts to write. He should do as much of his thinking as possible, before he writes. In this way he can 50 concentrate on the construction of his sentences. A rough but useful rule that students should bear in mind is—'Never write a sentence more than three lines in length.' The longer the sentence, of course, the greater is the chance of the writer making mistakes and failing to communicate the meaning. In particular the student should try to avoid a sentence with too many subordinate clauses.
55 Conversely—and a fourth cause of a breakdown in communication—the student

Margin annotations:
1- fail- collapse
2- unusual- strange
3- completly entirely
4- at least.
5- not to be relied on or trusted. possibly false.

127

may sometimes employ sentences which are too short and which are incomplete. For example, his sentence may lack a subject or a verb. The student, knowing the subject matter well himself, may think that he's conveyed his meaning quite clearly. The reader, however, remains confused.

60   The second main type of error is the error which—although it may only rarely lead to a breakdown in meaning—often irritates and sometimes momentarily may mislead the reader. The wrong selection of a verb tense frequently falls into this category. The student who writes, 'Before the second world war Einstein has discovered his famous formula $E = MC^2$', for example, makes a mistake which
65 doesn't interfere with the meaning. Often the student makes grammatical mistakes which fall into this second category and which he can correct himself if he checks his work sufficiently carefully. Then there are errors in concord: the subject and verb don't agree; errors in word order: the adverb has been placed in the wrong position; errors in article usage, particularly the omission of an article; all these frequently
70 occur in the work of the learner of English when he writes his essays or reports. When he writes, therefore, he should prepare several drafts. Each draft should be checked for the above points. If a student finds that he makes one type of mistake more often than others, then he should double check for that particular error. All this is, of course, time-consuming. There is, however, no substitute for it.
75   Finally, we come to the third type of error. This is the least damaging of the three, though it's still important. This type of error may be termed 'stylistic'. The English language, as you already know, is particularly rich in synonyms. However, these synonyms are not always inter-changeable: for instance, the two synonyms 'terrific' and 'impressive'. A student may, in conversation, hear someone say 'The results of
80 the research were terrific'. If he wants to convey the same meaning in a report, however, he must write 'The results of the research were most impressive'. The word 'terrific' is here restricted to a colloquial style even though in the sentence quoted above it means the same as 'most impressive'. Equally, the words 'area' and 'region'. A student may read about 'the northern area' or 'the northern region' of a country.
85 If he then sees a reference to 'an interesting area of research' he is likely to think that he can write 'an interesting region of research' as well. Unfortunately 'region' can't go with 'research'. The reader would understand what was meant by 'a region of research' but a native speaker of English would never express himself in this way.

Unit 8   Stage 1   Text

THE IMPORTANCE OF QUESTIONS

1 To obtain full value from a group discussion a student must be good at asking
2 questions. If his questions are not well-formed, misunderstandings are likely to
3 occur. In order to avoid these, a student should ensure that his teacher:
4   (a) knows that a question is intended
5   (b) understands the source of the difficulty
6   (c) is clear about the exact point involved.

Unit 8   Stage 1   Notes

(Figures in brackets refer to line numbers above.)

1   *PRONUNCIATION*
    (a) Note the rising intonation:

          (1) discussion

          (2) well-formed

          (3) these

        This intonation pattern is frequently used to signal that a clause (or sometimes an important phrase) has ended, but that the sentence will continue in order that the sense might be completed (e.g. with a purpose, result, consequence....). A short pause is often made at this point which may be represented in the written language by a comma.
    (b) In the title—/ɪmpɔtṇs/—importance
        line 1—/stjudṇt/—student
    note the dropping of the vowel in the unstressed syllable.
        (1).... must be
            ....exact point } the 't' is not released; the two words run into each other.
    (c) Note the '-ed' pronunciation:
        (2) well-formed, (6) involved—/d/
        (4) intended   —/ɪd/
        (Also: talked—/t/—which does not appear in this Stage.)

2   *STRUCTURE*
    (a) Two forms of the *purpose* clause:

          (1) To obtain full value from a group discussion
          (3) In order to avoid these
    (b) be + adj. + at + verb stem + ing + something
        (1/2) be good at asking questions
        (further e.g.s: be skilled at answering questions, be poor at joining in a discussion)
    (c) Note the 'reduced' relative clause:

          (6).... the exact point (which is) involved.

3   *VOCABULARY*
    (2) likely (= probably/expected)
    (3) ensure (= make sure/certain)
    (5) source (= basis/cause)
    (6) be clear about something (= fully understand)
    (6) involved (= implied/entailed/concerned)

Unit 8   Stage 2   Key to the Exercises

(Figures in brackets refer to line numbers in the Text in Exercise 2, located in the front section of the book.)

Exercise 1
1   T   (1–2)

2   T   (8–10)
3   F   (19–20)
4   F   (20–23)
5   T   (27–28)

Exercise 2

(2) at asking   (3) lead to   (5) whether   (5–6) at all   (6) as follows   (8) none on
(9) predictable   (11) with what   (12) even when   (13) arise   (14) the source
(15) was said   (16) have worked out   (17) these   (17) requires   (19) must ensure
(20) precise   (21) preface   (24) in a position   (26) exact point

Exercise 3

1   F   *Unfortunately* he (the student) concentrates all his attention on the subject
        matter and none on the language. (7–8)
2   T   .... he fails to employ the correct grammatical form .... The teacher inter-
        prets the intended question as a comment. (8–10)
3   F   .... even when the student does employ an appropriate question form,
        difficulties may still arise. (12–13)
4   T   In order to be absolutely precise, it's a good idea for students to preface
        their questions with an introductory statement .... (20–22)
5   T   The teacher is then [i.e. when he is clear about exactly which point he—the
        student—is referring to (19–20)] in a position to give a satisfactory
        answer .... (23–24)

Exercise 4

(a) *In order to be* absolutely precise, it's a good idea for students to preface their
    questions with an introductory statement .... (20–22)
(b) 1   **d**
    2   **e**
    3   **a**   in order to ⎫
    4   **c**   to   ⎬ may be used throughout
    5   **b**   so as to   ⎭
(c) suggested answers:
    1   Students should take notes so as to make revision easier.
    2   A student should read as widely as possible in order to increase his
        vocabulary.
    3   Students should check their written work carefully in order to avoid un-
        necessary mistakes.
    4   A student should use a language laboratory to improve his listening and
        speaking.
    5   Students should learn to use a library catalogue in order to find books
        quickly in the library.

Exercise 5

A number of questions are possible. Each one must begin with: 'Excuse me, please
could you ....', e.g.
1   Excuse me, please could you repeat the last sentence more loudly.
2   Excuse me, please could you explain the reference you made at the beginning
    about cost inflation.
3   Excuse me, please could you explain what you meant about the percentage
    involved.
4   Excuse me, please could you explain the reference about state planning.

5 Excuse me, please could you write the book title you gave on the blackboard.

NOTE:
The format of the questions in the table could be used in order to ask questions relating to the Stage 2 talk. At appropriate places in the talk the teacher could stop the tape and require students to ask appropriate questions.

Unit 8   Stage 3   Guided Note-taking

Suggested notes, completed in italic type.

<u>Title</u>: *Imp. of Qs.*
<u>Group discussions</u> = *valuable*
  BUT must be *proficient in asking Qs.*

  1 <u>In early stages *freq. breakdowns in commun.*</u>
      Explans.:   (i) *not a command — gram. & vocab.*
             (ii) *poor pron.*
             (iii) v. freq. cause = *st. asked Q.?*
                  — fails to *employ correct Q. form*
               e.g. *statement instead* →
                    teacher interprets Q. as comment

  2 <u>Even when st. employs approp. Q. form *diffs. may arise*</u>
    e.g. source *of st's diff.?*
        Differ. types: (a) *aural perception*
                   (b) *ling. knowledge*
                   (c) *subject matter*
        Each type reqs. *differ. kind of Qs.*

  3 <u>Q. must be *specific*</u>
    To be precise = *preface Qs. with intro. statement*
                 → Teacher in position *to give answer*
    Q. on text — *must locate exact point*

  4 <u>Correct Q. form imp.</u> — nec. not to be *rude*
      S'times *imperative instead of interrog.*
      Imp. ∴ *to practise Q. form*

New abbreviations used above:

Explans.	= explanations	*gram.*	= *grammar*
freq.	= frequent	*ling.*	= *linguistic*
approp.	= appropriate	*intro.*	= *introductory*
reqs.	= requires	*interrog.*	= *interrogative*
nec.	= necessary		

Unit 8   Stage 3   Text

THE IMPORTANCE OF QUESTIONS

Non-native speakers of English, like their native counterparts, usually find that the opportunity to participate in group discussions is one of the most valuable aspects in their whole academic programme. But in order to obtain full value from this type of activity the student must be proficient in asking questions. If he isn't, then any attempt to resolve his difficulties may lead to further confusion, if not considerable embarrassment.

Some students who are not fluent in the language find that in the early stages of their course there are frequent breakdowns in communication. There are, of course, many possible explanations for this. The student may not have a sufficient command over the grammar and vocabulary of English to enable him to express himself clearly. He may, on the other hand, have a poor pronunciation. Factors such as these, of course, require urgent and persistent attention on the part of the student. But a very frequent cause of misunderstanding in discussion sessions and one which can much more easily be put right, is the teacher's uncertainty whether his student has, in fact, asked a question at all. What often happens is as follows. The student, puzzled about a particular point, decides to ask a question. As so often happens when under pressure, he tends to concentrate most of his attention on the subject matter and he pays practically no attention to the language. Consequently he fails to employ the correct question form. For example, he may use a statement form instead. The result is predictable. The teacher interprets the intended question as a comment. He then either agrees or disagrees with it, or he continues with what he was saying before.

However, even when the student does employ an appropriate question form, difficulties may still arise. The teacher may not know, for example, what the source of the student's difficulty is. He may not be at all clear as to what he is really getting at. The basic difficulty may, in fact, be one of several different types. It may lie in the student's limited aural perception, in other words, the student may not have clearly heard what was said; or it may lie in his insufficient linguistic knowledge, that is to say, he may not have understood the English that his teacher employed; or alternatively, it may lie in his lack of knowledge of the subject matter itself, i.e. he may not have worked out the meaning of a point in relation to his special subject. Each type of difficulty requires a different kind of question. If the student, for example, does not clearly specify that his difficulty is that he did not quite catch what was said, then the teacher is quite likely to give an explanation in terms of the subject matter. All that is really necessary in such cases is a simple repetition of the original statement.

Next, a student must ensure that his teacher is clear about exactly which point he is referring to. To put it in another way, the question must be specific. Many native speakers make mistakes in this area, too. They ask questions which are too broad and which require supplementary questions before getting to the point. In order to be absolutely precise, it is a good idea if students preface their questions with an introductory statement. They might say, for example, something like the following: 'I don't understand the point you made at the beginning of the discussion about cost inflation. Could you explain it again please.' The teacher is always in a position to give a satisfactory answer to this form of question without any waste of time. He knows what type of difficulty the student has—one of subject matter. He knows precisely where the difficulty occurs—at the beginning of the discussion. And he knows precisely what point the student refers to—cost inflation.

Perhaps, before concluding, one further example may be helpful. When a student is given the opportunity to ask questions on a text, he must be particularly careful to locate the exact point. Thus, 'Page 3, three lines from the top, the word "straightforward". Would you explain it to me please', is clearly a better question than the utterance of the single word 'straightforward' (on a rising intonation)

which leaves the teacher to work out the reference and the nature of the difficulty.
55 All this is, of course, common sense, but it is surprising how often students ignore it.

Finally, one point that should be mentioned before we leave this subject. The correct use of the question form is important for another reason than basic communication. It is often necessary to employ it because not to do so would be rude. The non-native speaker is normally well aware of this, but when he is nervous and
60 is struggling with new subject-matter in a foreign language, he may sometimes find himself using the imperative instead of the interrogative form. Learners of English have, for example, said to me such things as 'See me here tomorrow' or 'Explain this'. Fortunately, as I deal with non-native speakers and as I understand their language problems, I interpret this as inadequacy in the language rather than
65 rudeness. Other teachers, however, may feel angry at receiving such orders. It is important, therefore, to practise the necessary question forms in order to avoid such problems.

Unit 9   Stage 1   Text

GROUP DISCUSSIONS

1 In an academic context, group discussions are often called 'seminars' and 'tutorials'.
2 Originally there were clear differences in size and in purpose between a seminar and
3 a tutorial. Nowadays these terms are often interchanged.
4   Group discussions have two main aims: to discuss students' difficulties and to
5 enable lecturers and students to have more personal contact.
6   Students find discussion work particularly difficult. There are a number of reasons
7 for this.

Unit 9   Stage 1   Notes

(Figures in brackets refer to line numbers above.)

1 *PRONUNCIATION*
   There are several examples of the final consonant sound in a word not being fully pronounced but running into the first consonant sound of the following word. Listen carefully to these examples:

   (1) academic context   (1) & (4) group discussions
   (4) discuss students'   (6) find discussion work particularly

2 *STRUCTURE*
   (a) (1) . . . . are often called seminars
       (3) . . . . are often interchanged
       Note the use of the passive, also the position of the adverb of frequency ('often'), i.e. before the verb stem (see Unit 2, Exercise 5).
   (b) (2) . . . . differences in size   } i.e. way in which items are compared (other
                  purpose)   examples: weight, quality . . . .)
       (2/3) (differences) between a seminar and a tutorial—i.e. items being compared
   (c) (2) There were clear differences . . . . }
       (6) There are a number of reasons . . . . } Examples of 'introductory' there.

       If a speaker wishes to explain simply that something *exists* or *occurs*, the most common construction to use is 'there is/are . . . .'.

133

3   *VOCABULARY*
  (1) context (= situation)
  (3) Nowadays (= at the present time; in these days/times)
  (3) terms (= words/expressions)
  (5) enable (= make it possible for someone to do something, cf. 'ensure' in Unit 8, Stage 1)

Unit 9   Stage 2   Key to the Exercises

(Figures in brackets refer to line numbers in the Text in Exercise 2, located in the front section of the book.)

Exercise 1
1   T   (1–2)
2   F   (8)
3   F   (12–13)
4   F   (14–20)
5   T   (23–24)

Exercise 2
(1) I'd like   (3) these terms   (4) I'll mention   (7) there were   (8) two to five
(9) asked and   (10) whereas   (11) served as   (13) for both   (15) objectives
(16) be helped   (17) arising from   (18) aren't   (19) quote again   (21) much easier
(22) they're   (24) of them   (25) for this   (26) the dialogue   (27) major

Exercise 3
1   F   Firstly....(2), then....(3) and finally....(4)
2   F   ....finally I'll *mention* some of the problems learners of English may have in work of this kind. (4–5)
3   F   Originally....a seminar was attended by about ten to fifteen (8–9)....in a seminar one student would usually give a short talk....(10–11)
4   F   The main aim is that....'students should be helped to discuss and to clarify difficulties arising from lectures or other teaching sessions'. (15–17)
5   F   There are *many reasons* for this (i.e. the difficulty). I'll just mention three.... (24–25)

Exercise 4
(a)   (ii) firstly (6), Firstly (26), Secondly (26)
      (iii) NIL
      (iv) Therefore (13)
      (v) However (12), Yet (23)
(b)   (i) therefore
      (ii) However etc.
      (iii) Therefore
      (iv) moreover etc.
(c) Many answers are possible. Suggestions:
      1   However, the students were able to make good notes.
      2   Nevertheless, three students managed to ask satisfactory questions.
      3   Furthermore, it contained useful summaries at the end of each chapter.
      4   Thus, there were no errors in the final draft.

Exercise 5

(a) In a tutorial a lecturer asked and answered questions related to his recent lecture whereas in a seminar one student would usually give a short talk which served as an introduction to a more general discussion. (9–12)

(b) Many answers are possible. Suggestions:

1 An encyclopedia will be found in the reference section of a library whereas a text-book will be found in the lending section.

2 The Contents are to be found at the front of a book while the Index is to be found at the back.

3 Whereas a footnote may appear at the bottom of a page, the title will appear at the top.

4 In a lecture the lecturer will speak for most of the time whereas in a seminar the students may speak most of the time.

5 An essay is normally a short piece of writing on a subject while a thesis is a very long one.

Unit 9   Stage 3   Guided Note-taking

Suggested notes, completed in italic type.

Title: *Group discussions*

In acad. context = *seminars & tutorials*

    1 *meaning of terms*   2 *aims*
    3 *probs.*   4 *advice*

1 Terms — trad. differs. = (i) *size of group*
                          (ii) *purpose*
    Tut. = *small: 2–5 sts.*   Sem. = *larger: 10–15*
    Tut. = *lecturer asked & answered Qs. on lecture*
          + essay/report?
    Sem. = *discuss prev. arranged topic*
          1st pres. paper + disc.
    Survey in *1967* by Dr. Ruth Beard *at London Univ.*
    → some lecturers use *2 words interchangeably*
    ∴ using 'group disc.'

2 Two most *imp. objectives*
        (i) *sts. discuss & clarify diffs. from lectures, etc.*
        (ii) *intimate & pers. contact with sts.*
        Other aims: (a) *oral pres. of reports*
                      (b) *promote logical thinking*   etc.

3 Diffs. — imp.:
        (i) *speed of dialogue*
        (ii) *break into disc.? — ling. formulae*
        (iii) *formulate Qs. quickly & accurately*
        (iv) *psycho. attitude — shy/uncomfortable?*

4 Advice:
        (i) *Build up self-confidence — learn lang. forms*
           & put into practice

135

(ii) Altho' gram. accuracy IS imp., *ability to commun.*
  orally = 1st objective

New abbreviations used above:

acad. = academic

trad. = traditional

tut. = tutorial

sem. = seminar

Altho' = although

prev.   = previously

pres.   = presented/presentation

disc.   = discussion

pers.   = personal

psycho. = psychological

commun. = communicate

Unit 9   Stage 3   Text

GROUP DISCUSSIONS

Today I'd like to talk to you about group discussions which, in an academic context, are usually known as 'seminars' and 'tutorials'. I want first of all to deal with the meaning of these terms, then I want to cover the aims of group discussions; next I'll go on to look at some problems that learners of English are likely to experience
5 in work of this kind; and then finally I'd like to offer a few pieces of advice.

Firstly, then, let's look at the meaning of the terms 'seminar' and 'tutorial'. Nowadays it's becoming more and more difficult to draw a precise distinction between the meaning of the two words that all lecturers would be willing to accept. The traditional differences which are still accepted by many lecturers, are firstly the
10 size of the group and secondly, and perhaps more importantly, their purpose. A tutorial was usually for a small number of students, say between two and five, whereas a seminar was attended by a larger group, say between ten and fifteen. In a tutorial a lecturer or tutor adopted the role of the expert and asked and answered questions related to his most recent lecture. Often a student had to submit an essay
15 or a report which was discussed by the tutor and then by other members of the tutorial group. In short, the tutor took the lead; he in fact 'tutored'. The purpose of the seminar, on the other hand, was to provide an opportunity to discuss a previously arranged topic. More than one member of staff might be present and one of them would probably act as chairman. Often one student presented a paper, that
20 is, gave a short talk which served as an introduction to a more general discussion. The other students may have been asked to read a number of chapters of a book, related to the talk, so as to be in a better position to participate in the discussion.

These are, as I've pointed out, the traditional distinctions drawn between seminars and tutorials. However, a survey carried out in 1967 by Dr. Ruth Beard at London
25 University has shown that some lecturers use the two words interchangeably or even reverse the meanings. Consequently she suggests using the term 'group discussion' for either. From now on I also intend to use 'group discussion' to cover both 'tutorial' and 'seminar'.

Let's now turn to the general aims of group discussions. I want to mention the
30 two most important objectives which emerged from the survey at London University; afterwards I'll mention a few more specific objectives.

In the first place, the aim which far outweighs all others in importance is that, and I quote, 'students should be helped to discuss and to clarify difficulties arising from lectures or other teaching sessions'. It should be remembered that lectures are
35 usually fairly formal and students are not really expected to interrupt the lecturer

136

to ask a question or to disagree with a point he's made. It's usual to wait for the follow-up group discussion to ask questions or challenge a lecturer's points.

The second most important objective is, and I quote again, 'to obtain more intimate and personal contact with students than is possible in lectures'. Very often lectures
40　are attended by a relatively large number of students and it's virtually impossible for the lecturer to give students personal attention. The discussion sessions, in smaller groups, provide this opportunity.

Other more specific aims mentioned by Dr. Beard include: to give practice in oral presentation of reports; to promote critical and logical thinking; to ensure that
45　concepts and principles are understood and to provide feedback to staff on students' progress.

Group discussions of any type, are a demanding part of any academic course and, if properly exploited by students, can be highly stimulating and extremely beneficial. Yet many students, especially non-native speakers, understandably find it
50　difficult to take full advantage of them. There are many reasons for this. I'll just mention four which I think are particularly important.

Firstly, there's the speed of the dialogue. This is especially the case if the student finds he's the only non-native speaker in a group. If there's a rapid interchange between two or more native speakers it may well prove difficult for the learner of
55　English to follow with ease. Secondly, a non-native speaker may not know how to break into a discussion by drawing attention to himself politely: unfortunately it's easy to create the wrong impression by using, for instance, an unsuitable opening phrase or by choosing an inappropriate intonation pattern. Furthermore, the student may be unaware of the acceptable linguistic formulae used to express disagreement,
60　to ask for an explanation or to interrupt another student. The third major difficulty is how to formulate questions quickly and accurately: it often happens that a student has something to ask but by the time he's mentally worked out the form of his question the discussion has moved on to another topic and his chance has gone. Fourthly, there's the psychological attitude towards discussions: a student who comes
65　to Britain to study and finds himself in the company of predominantly British students might feel, at least initially, shy to the point of feeling uncomfortable. This can be a big problem for students who are already shy and reserved by nature. If these feelings are combined with a sense of linguistic inferiority it may make it even harder to take part in group discussions.

70　So what advice can be given to learners of English who have difficulty in participating in group discussions? Well, it's not easy. Unfortunately—and this applies to all aspects of language learning—there's no magic formula which, when learnt, solves the problem overnight. However, the first thing to do is to try to build up self-confidence. This can only be done by learning the language forms commonly
75　used by native speakers to ask questions, interrupt, disagree, ask for explanation etc. and then by taking every opportunity to put them into practice. Practise putting questions to your teacher and to your fellow students; practise also asking for a point to be explained in greater detail; practise disagreeing with others' points of view. This will definitely help you overcome any shyness you may have. Secondly,
80　you should realize that although grammatical accuracy is important, the ability to communicate orally must be your first objective, even if you're not using perfectly correct English constructions. So try to make a contribution to group discussions even though you may not be so sure of your grammar.

Unit 10   Stage 1   Text

LEARNING A LANGUAGE

1 For this last talk in this series of lectures I'm going to discuss learning a language.
2 I shall deal with the basic problems first and then I'll go on to suggest various
3 possible solutions. The students I have in mind here are those who have been learning
4 English in order to begin a course of studies taught in that medium.

Unit 10   Stage 1   Notes

(Figures in brackets refer to line numbers above.)

1   *PRONUNCIATION*
Notice the amount of stress put on some words—especially groups of words
where an extra strong stress seems to be put on each word. This is deliberate
and indicates that each strongly stressed word is of considerable importance to
the meaning.
viz. (1) *learning a language*
    (2) *basic problems first*
    (2/3) *various possible solutions*
    (4) *taught in that medium*

2   *STRUCTURE*
This short talk contains a number of grammatical constructions that have been
referred to in previous Units, e.g.

    (1) learning = a gerund
    (2) then = connective (enumeration)
    (3) The students I have in mind . . . . = reduced relative clause
    (3) those who . . . . = relative clause
    (4) in order to begin . . . . = purpose clause

3   *VOCABULARY*
    (1) series (= number of things coming one after the other)
      this series = 'series' is a countable noun and has the same spelling for both
            singular and plural forms. Here 'series' is singular (it can be used
            with 'a' as well as 'this').
    (3) *I have in mind* = as a matter of *style* this is more appropriate to the *spoken*
            language. In the written language, more formally, probably
            'I want to refer to' would be used.

Unit 10   Stage 2   Key to the Exercises

(Figures in brackets refer to line numbers in the Text in Exercise 2, located in the
front section of the book.)

Exercise 1
1   F   (1–2)
2   T   (7–8)
3   T   (11–13)
4   F   (14–16)
5   T   (21–23)

Exercise 2

(1) series of   (3) I'll go on   (4) have been   (5) taught   (6) meets   (7) too
(8) student's   (10) fails to   (11) moreover   (12) in areas   (14) enough
(17) All of this   (18) anxious   (19) one's   (21) can be   (21) there are
(23) deal with them   (23) must set   (24) targets   (26) encourage

Exercise 3

1   F   .... those who have been learning English in order to *begin* a course of studies
        taught in that medium. (3–5)
2   F   .... the feeling that the problem is *too* great for him. (7)
3   F   .... his social relations are difficult as he cannot always find the right phrase
        quickly enough to keep a conversation going. (13–14)
4   F   .... the concentration and self-discipline required to correct one's mistakes
        is *very* great indeed. (18–20)
5   F   .... the student must set himself a number of *realistic* targets. (23–24)

Exercise 4

(a) 1   .... the problem is *too* great for him (=excess) (7)
    2   .... he can*not* always find the right phrase quickly *enough* .... (insufficiency)
        (13–14)
(b) 1   b   (c) 2   not precise enough
    2   e   3   carefully enough
    3   f   4   too *much* pressure
    4   c   5   too ambitious
    5   d   6   positive enough
    6   a

Exercise 5

1   a   —   When/student
2   seems (or: appears)   —   sometimes/to
3   too   —   are/great
4   language   —   the/seems
5   While (or: Whereas)   —   student./Seminars
6   native   —   the/speaker
7   to   —   likely/find
8   not   —   is/skilful
9   from   —   benefit/these
10 of   —   area/language
11 as   —   so/to
12 problems (or: difficulties)   —   any/he

Unit 10   Stage 3   Guided Note-taking

Suggested notes, completed in italic type.

Title: *Learning a lang.*
    1   Basic probs.
    2   *Poss. solutions*

1   Most fund. prob. = *feeling probs. too great*
    Now Eng. = med. of instr. →
        — unknown *gram. & vocab.*

— diffs. with *subject matter*
— reading *slows down & compre. less secure*   etc. etc.
— social relations = *diff.*
Lang. seems *in control of st.*   etc.

2   St. can help self:
    (1)   *realistic targets*
    (2)   *method of study*
    (3)   *set of attitudes — progress*
 (1)   Targets — REALISTIC! = most imp. → immed. short-term:
      Personal = *regard to st's. own ability*
     Proximate = go for next stage not perfection
       Precise = define immed. objective exactly
    e.g. Every day *learn 6 words in special subject*
 (2)   Method — systematic, thoro', econ. *& flex.*
    e.g. *vocab. — note-book — words*
     Write: (i)   *whole sentence*
          (ii)   *meaning in Eng.*
          (iii)   ,,   ,, *own lang.* (optional)
     Learned 3 ways:
          (i)   *repetition*
          (ii)   mnemonic *devices*
          (iii)   *integrating relationships*
            'eventually' = pract. e.g.
     St. should *look at note-book during day*
     — daily *self-testing*
 (3)   Progress in lang. = most likely if *st. develops*
    interest in for. lang. community

New abbrevations used above:

fund.	= fundamental	immed.	= immediate
med.	= medium	thoro'	= thorough
instr.	= instruction	pract.	= practical
compre.	= *comprehension*	*econ.*	= *economical*
		flex.	= *flexible*

Unit 10   Stage 3   Text

LEARNING A LANGUAGE

For this last talk in this series of lectures I'm going to discuss learning a language. I shall deal with the basic problems first and then I'll go on to suggest various possible solutions. The students I have in mind here are those who've been learning English in order to begin a course of studies taught in that medium.

5   Probably the most fundamental problem that the student meets is the feeling that the problem is too great for him. Difficulties occur on all sides and progress can be uncertain and slow. In the past, learning English as a *separate subject* seemed relatively easy. The text book selected and graded items of language which were put into contexts and then practised intensively. New items were carefully controlled
10   so that the student could cope quite easily. Now that English is used as a medium of instruction, however, all this changes. Unknown items of grammar and vocabulary

appear in texts which attempt to explain new and often difficult information. Difficulties with the language interact with difficulties as regards the subject matter. The student's reading in his own subject slows down, and his comprehension becomes less secure. He expresses himself slowly and often fails to convey his ideas exactly. He's disappointed to find that under pressure he makes a lot of unnecessary mistakes in areas where he knows the correct language forms. His social relations are difficult as he cannot find the right phrase quickly enough to keep a conversation going, so his language often betrays him into dullness, coldness, or worst of all rudeness. Instead of the student being in control of the language, the language seems now to be in control of the student.

All of this can be very depressing and the student can start to feel very anxious. Working in a foreign language is also very tiring, and the concentration and self-discipline required to correct one's mistakes is very great indeed.

But what can be done about these problems? Well, there are many ways in which the student can help himself. It might be helpful if we deal with them under three broad headings. Firstly, the student must set himself a number of realistic targets. Secondly, he must work out an appropriate method of study. Thirdly, he must try to adopt a set of attitudes which encourage progress.

First then, the targets. You'll recall that I said that they should be 'realistic'. This is *most* important. As we have seen the student naturally compares performance in his own language with that in the foreign language. What he does not appreciate sufficiently is that the performance he achieves in his own language is the result of learning over a whole life-time; the performance in the foreign language is the result of maybe several hundred hours of classroom instruction. Bearing this in mind the student must concentrate on immediate short-term improvements rather than vague long-term aims. Targets, or objectives, should be personal, proximate and precise. Personal, proximate, and precise. What do we mean by this? By saying targets should be *personal* we mean that they should be set with due regard to realistic estimates of the student's own ability. By saying they should be *proximate* (note the spelling by the way: p-r-o-x-i-m-a-t-e)—by saying they should be proximate—we mean that the student should go first of all for the next stage and not aim straight away for ultimate perfection. By saying targets should be *precise*, we mean that the student should define the immediate objective as exactly as he can. A practical example may be helpful here. The student should, if he has a problem as regards vocabulary, not say 'I'll learn as many words as possible to-morrow' but rather 'Every day, starting to-day, I'll learn six new words which occur frequently in my special subject'. Six words should not present too many problems. If it does, the number can be lowered; if it presents no problems, the number can be raised. The aim, too, is one which allows the student to build up his vocabulary in limited stages, i.e. it's *proximate*, and it defines what type of words are to be learned, i.e. it's *precise*.

Next, though, we must consider the appropriate method of study. This should be systematic, thorough, economical, and flexible. It may be helpful if we again illustrate this from our example of vocabulary building. A good idea is to keep a pocket note-book and note down in it the words which are not understood. Three items of information may be written against each word: firstly, the whole sentence (or the relevant clause) in which it appears; secondly, the meaning as given in a good English dictionary (preferably one specially written for foreign students); and thirdly, the meaning in translation in the student's own language. This last item is optional and should perhaps only be used in the earlier stages when confidence needs to be built up. It may also be used if there's uncertainty about the meaning of the English definition. The aim should be to cut out translation as early as possible. In this way the student accelerates the process by which he can *think* easily and fluently in the language.

65 Having noted these three items, they then have to be learned. In the final analysis there are perhaps only three ways in which the meaning of a word can be learned: by repetition, by the use of mnemonic devices, by working out the integrating relationships. Let's take the word 'eventually' as a practical example. Repetition— where the student merely says over and over again 'eventually means x',—can some-

70 times be helpful but unless the need to learn is very urgent, the mind quickly begins to wander, and only a small amount of learning takes place. The student sometimes works out a mnemonic, that's to say a special device or technique to help him remember. He may notice for example that the first letter for the word in his own language begins with the same first letter in the English word. Lastly, there's the

75 attempt to work out an integrating relationship. The original context from which the word is taken may help here, or if this is insufficiently helpful, the student may construct another context from a relevant personal experience. He might write in his notebook 'At first I got bad marks in my economics, but eventually I became top of my group.'

80 The student should look at his note-book at odd moments during the day and make use of each of these learning techniques. A system of daily self-testing should also be devised: one which moreover includes a technique for dealing with those words which still cause problems even after all these steps have been taken.

Finally, there is the question of positive attitudes towards language learning.

85 Progress in the language is most likely to be achieved if the student develops a general interest in the foreign language community. The student should, therefore, involve himself as much as possible with the foreign culture, and should seek out opportunities to enjoy himself through it. Such enjoyment always makes language learning quicker and more effective.

KEY AND NOTES TO THE FOLLOW-UP ACTIVITIES

Unit 3   Stage 3   Follow-up Activity 1

1   (i) 1. Understanding what the lecturer says as he says it.
          2. Deciding what is important.
          3. Writing down the main points.
          4. Showing connections between points.
    (ii) Try to infer their meaning from the context.
    (iii) Because it is often possible to understand much of a lecture by concentrating on the main points.
    (iv) Signals are used to help the listener decide what is important. A direct signal explicitly tells the listeners that a point is important and that they should write it down. An indirect signal indicates that a point is important by the use of slower or louder speech or a greater range of intonation.
    (v)   They help the listener decide when to write. Connectives such as 'moreover', 'also' etc. indicate that an additional point (i.e. under the same heading) is being made and that it is, therefore, a safe time to write. The student should listen carefully when s/he hears connectives such as 'however', 'on the other hand', etc. because they usually introduce new/unexpected information.
    (vi) To use a visual presentation, i.e. spacing, underlining, numbering points and employing conventional symbols.

Unit 3   Stage 3   Follow-up Activity 2

1   (i)   Today I'd like to talk about . . . (Unit 1)
           Today I'm going to analyse . . . (Unit 3)
    (ii)   I'll comment only briefly on . . . and then spend most of the time looking at . . . (Unit 1)
           (Let's look at this) in some detail . . . (Unit 1)
           I'll just mention three (Unit 1)
           . . . (I'd like to mention) briefly (Unit 2)
           . . . which I haven't the time to discuss in detail . . . (Unit 2)
    (iii) . . . also . . . (×3: Unit 1), (Unit 2), (×3: Unit 3)
           Secondly . . . (×2: Unit 1), (Unit 2)
           Thirdly . . . (Unit 1), (Unit 2)
           Perhaps most important of all . . . (Unit 1) (*Note:* this also indicates relative importance*)
           Furthermore . . . (Unit 2)
           Finally . . . (Unit 2)
           Other (factors) . . . include . . . (Unit 2)
           An important . . . is . . .* (Unit 3)
           . . . too (Unit 3)
    (iv)   Looking now at . . . (Unit 1)
           Let's look at this . . . (Unit 1)
           What can a student do then to . . .? (Unit 1)
           The (advice) here . . . (Unit 1)
           Let's examine . . . (Unit 2)

But I want to now come on to . . . (Unit 2)
Thirdly I want to deal with . . . (Unit 2)
Why is this? I'll suggest . . . (Unit 2)
There are, however, other (problems) . . . I'd like to mention (briefly) (Unit 2)
But how does the student . . .? It is, in fact, the second . . . I want to talk about today . . . (Unit 3)
. . . however . . . This is, in fact, the third . . . (Unit 3)
The fourth . . . (Unit 3) (*Note:* sequencers, i.e. Firstly, secondly, etc., the first, the second etc. are used to introduce both a further point under the same heading and a new part of the talk, i.e. under the same title.)

(v) For example . . . (× 2: Unit 1), (Unit 2), (Unit 3)
e.g. (× 2: Unit 1)
Such . . . include . . . (Unit 1)
For instance . . . (Unit 2)
To give an example . . . (Unit 2)
Other . . . include . . . (Unit 2)
. . . are examples of this (Unit 3)
. . . such as . . . (Unit 3)

(vi) * Perhaps most important of all . . . (Unit 1)
It's worth noticing . . . (Unit 2)
It's worth remembering that (Unit 3)
An important . . . is . . . (Unit 3)

(vii) . . . in other words . . . (× 2: Unit 1)
By . . . I mean . . . (Unit 2)

Unit 6   Stage 3   Follow-up Activity 1

1   (i) (a) Class number = subject area (Dewey Decimal System)
i.e. Tells the student which general area in the library to go to in order to find the book.

(b) Author number: Capital letter = first letter of author's surname
: Number = name
: Small letter (in some systems) = first letter of title of book
i.e. Directs the student to the exact shelf.

(ii) (a) They give details of the publisher, and place and date of publication.
(b) They give the number of volumes, pages, illustrations and maps.

(iii) (a) an encyclopedia
(b) a specialized bibliography
(c) the relevant professional journals

(iv) To avoid the risk of spending too much time in the coffee bar, thereby using the library as a social rather than a study centre.

Unit 8   Stage 3   Follow-up Activity 2

A text of approximately 500 words is suggested for this exercise in order to provide sufficient scope for questions. The lines may be numbered although, clearly, the exercise is more challenging linguistically if they are not.

The level of difficulty and subject-matter is at the individual teacher's/student's discretion.